Using Their Brains
in Science

Using Their Brains in Science

Ideas for Children Aged 5 to 14

Hellen Ward

P·C·P

Paul Chapman
Publishing

Paul Chapman Publishing
P·C·P A SAGE Publications Company
  1 Oliver's Yard
  55 City Road
  London EC1Y 1SP

SAGE Publications Inc
2455 Teller Road
Thousand Oaks, California 91320

SAGE Publications India Pvt Ltd
B 1/I 1 Mohan Cooperative Industrial Area
Mathura Road
New Delhi 110 044

SAGE Publications Asia-Pacific Pte Ltd
33 Pekin Street #02-01
Far East Square
Singapore 048763

Library of Congress Control Number: 2007934639

British Library Cataloguing in Publication Data
A catalogue record for this book is available from the British Library

ISBN 978-1-4129-4663-6
ISBN 978-1-4129-4664-3 (pbk)

Typeset by Dorwyn, Wells, Somerset
Printed in Great Britain by T.J. International, Padstow, Cornwall
Printed on paper from sustainable resources

Contents

About the author

Hellen Ward is actively involved in science education, working as a science senior lecturer at Canterbury Christ Church University and with teachers in a number of local authorities. Hellen has written several books and a number of other publications, and has developed teaching resources and teaching materials to support the teaching and learning of science. She has also contributed to science television programmes, website and teaching resources for the BBC and the teacher training resource bank (www.ttrb.ac.uk). Hellen is Programme Director for Modular PGCE at Christ Church and is also an independent education consultant. Hellen is an active member of the Association for Science Education (ASE). She is a regional secretary and a regular contributor to both national and regional conferences. She is also a member of the Association for Achievement and Improvement through Assessment (AIAA) and has published materials on assessment.

Acknowledgements

This book would not have been completed without the help and support of many learners, teachers and headteachers. I would like to thank particularly Peter Hellman and the staff and pupils at Senacre Wood Primary School, Katrina Ware and the staff and children of Bobbing Village School, Maureen King and the children of Elphinstone Primary School and Caroline Weston and the children of Guestling Bradshaw Primary School.

Thanks also go to Hugh Ritchie (who is skilled with a camera and is responsible for the photographs), to John Armstrong, my father, for the excellent artwork and to Keith Remnant, my husband, for his support and Charlotte for her editing and indexing skills.

Hellen Ward

Introduction

The idea for this book has developed from working in classrooms with many teachers and learners and through listening to what they say. Teachers worry that learners forget what is taught whilst the learners ask such questions as 'Shall I underline the title?', 'Do you want the long date or short date?' and 'Is this right?' A greater understanding of how learners' brains work should make it easier to promote good learning. Perhaps today too much time is focused on strategies and systems and on the structure of the curriculum, instead of on how quality learning happens.

'Why is it important to understand how the brain works?'

One answer could be that it is not important and it is merely enough for teachers to know what to teach. This approach has its limits, as without an understanding of how the brain works teaching will not equate to learning. So 'How it is taught?' is as important as 'What is taught!' Teaching is a demanding activity and meeting the needs of 30 learners takes considerable time and energy. Coping with the demands of day-to-day teaching can preclude any thoughts about the bigger picture and the purpose of education. Is teaching today about enabling learners to fit into the world as it is now or about providing them with the knowledge, understanding and skills that will enable them to be active participants in a rapidly changing world? Change is happening fast and is signalled by increasing technological advances; mobile phones being used by five year-olds is now not such a strange thought, teenagers who can text faster than they can put on their shoes, the opportunity to 'pod cast' radio and television programmes, the ability to pause and delay a live television broadcast to suit our 'time and needs', are only a few aspects of the early twenty first century. It is an increasingly different world and therefore easy to bemoan the loss of a childhood which those of us who are adults once knew.

As the world develops and changes it is important in education that these new technologies bring new learning opportunities, but also provide learners with greater knowledge and understanding about what is occurring. These new technologies and knowledge need to be used to amend and improve methods of teaching and learning. ICT Throughout this book ICT has been selectively used, so there is no individual chapter on this area as it is treated as a teaching tool which is useful throughout and not as a stand-alone extra. To help you to identify quickly where ICT would make a contribution to science teaching an ICT icon has been placed in the margin. There is a suggestion that the body of science knowledge now doubles every five years (QCA, 2005). If this is true then should this have an impact on teaching? Should a knowledge of science still be what is most important, or will there be an even greater need to develop learners' basic skills and understanding in order for them to make greater sense of the world in which they live and have responsibility for?

This book hopes to illuminate the discussion. It is not a theoretical book but starts with theory to provide a framework for the suggestions and activities. Chapter 1 begins with an outline of the brain and how it works. The focus here is on the whole process of thinking and learning rather than on what happens in different parts of the brain. Chapter 2 focuses on learning, motivation and memory, all vital if what is taught is to be made use of. Chapter 3 brings a detective approach to science. Investigative and problem-solving approaches are central to this chapter. Moving and learning, in Chapter 4, looks to drama as a way of developing links in the brain, as well as providing opportunities for modelling using the learner's body. This chapter develops key ideas but is only a starting point. Children's vocabulary is an area which teachers will always want to develop further. Chapter 5 starts with the way in which language is learned and explores the immense capability the brain has for developing language, then suggests activities, ideas and opportunities that will support the development of scientific language in the classroom. Writing in science is taken as a chapter on its own and includes ideas for investigative work which are illustrated by selected examples. Assessing science is vital if learners are to reach their capabilities and assessment for learning is therefore central to Chapter 7. The book ends by using examples from schools as a starting point to review creativity. Overall the aim is to inspire teachers rather than provide a template for creative lessons.

1

Understanding how the brain works

The way the brain works fascinates many scientists, however much of what is known about the brain and its working has been discovered within the last fifteen years. It is a collection of cells that control all thoughts, words and deeds. Greenfield (1995: 22) asked, 'How does our state of consciousness derive from the slurry of tissues that have the consistency of a boiled egg?' It is strange to think that this very mass of tissue is someone's individuality! The brain is made up of neurons and generally its size is related to the size of the animal concerned; therefore, the bigger the animal the bigger the brain. However, it is not the number of neurons on their own that is important; for instance, an octopus has three times as many neurons as the average human.[1] When working the brain is said to be in a state of arousal; the amount of arousal differs and only ceases at death. Our brain is central to learning and understanding.

Understanding is a personal thing and while it is not possible to teach understanding (Newton, 2000), it is possible to help learners gain understanding by the teaching methods selected. There are some things that can be taught without understanding such as a simple set of instructions or the names of the seven processes of life, these can be learned by rote. This does not grant a deep understanding of what the life processes are or provide the ability to relate them to other contexts. This was evidenced by a Key Stage 2 science paper in the 2002 national tests, where children were asked, 'Which one life process can an adult do that a young child cannot?' The required or expected

---

[1] It is not the number but the way they link together that is most important. Those in humans are linked in many different ways. This will be developed later in this chapter.

response was, 'Adults can reproduce'. However, many children gave different responses such as: 'going to a nightclub', 'staying up late', 'drinking and smoking'. Although many children knew of the seven processes, most were unable to make the link in the context provided. It is possible to argue that the children were thinking both in a scientific and everyday way. Indeed a number of research projects have found that children revert to experiences from everyday life to make sense of some scientific questions. A key point from this example is that in order to help learners in science, teaching has to take account of how they learn and doing this effectively requires an understanding of the role of the brain in the process.

Children do not make gains in learning in isolation and successes can be affected by many factors. These might include social and/or environmental factors, for example, something that happens as they enter the classroom. The relevance they attach to these incidents, to what they being are taught and also to their prior knowledge, understanding and experience of what is intended, will all impact upon their self-esteem and motivation and thus could affect learning. In a world of strategies, sound bites and quick fixes, it is useful to start with some key facts about learning:

• it is often hard and sometimes painful
• progress is rarely linear
• all learners are different
• what is taught may be buried, altered and/or ignored
• real learning is challenging and takes time and practice.

Riding a bike is something that many children learn to do. For many it does not come quickly or easily, it often needs courage because of the pain involved when they fall off. The process requires them to put together many complex skills and to develop the confidence that they will achieve. In the early stages many children also need to have confidence in the person holding the bike. However, with practice and encouragement most children learn to coordinate themselves a bicycle and some even learn to ride 'without hands'. How does this happen and is it the same as learning other skills:

Cells called neurons

Mankind has come a long way in understanding the mind, from the early Greeks who thought that the lungs were where it all happened, to a focus on the brain that occurred by the end of the sixth century

BC. It is known that the brain is made up of neurons. These are cells, which are invisible to the naked eye but are not as small as atoms. Neurons are the building blocks of learning. The human brain consists of a mass of a hundred million cells that, when working or aroused, release electricity and tiny amounts of chemicals. So far, no-one has discovered any chemical unique to the brain. It does not stop making connections even when a person is asleep or anesthetised. During these states the brain is working at a much-reduced rate; it is said there is little arousal. Therefore arousal is not the same as consciousness. The brain is always making links – the difference is in the degree of working and therefore it is permanently aroused.

The fact that neurons can generate electrical signals makes them different from all other cells in the body. Galvani, an early scientist who was a doctor and physicist, discovered in 1783 that nerve cells conducted electricity. His discovery was developed further by Volta to produce the first battery and from this electricity, as it is used today, was developed. However, the idea of electricity and its effect in the body was not advanced until 1950. Thereafter it was found that it was neurons that generated electricity and that this could be transferred from one neuron to the next. Electrical activity in the first neuron results in a release of chemicals that then act on the next neuron, thus causing a change in the electrical activity, which in turn affects the next neuron – and so a chain of electrical and chemical action is built up. Although there is nothing special about the chemicals, they are also found in other parts of the body; the chemicals and electrical signals working together form the basis for thought, learning and creativity. These electrical impulses are found to some extent in the brain cells of many living things, but in the human brain these simple chemicals and impulses cause thoughts and thinking about thinking.[2]

The brain has separate sections that can be seen with the naked eye. It is known that some functions of the brain are located in specific areas, however many functions happen throughout the brain and are not limited to a single place. Greenfield (1995: 27) found that the function relating to sight is located in as many as 30 places throughout the brain. Scientists now use Magnetic Resonance Imaging (MRI scanning) to gain information about the working of the brain, but in the early 1800s Flourens provided scientific evidence that some functions occur in all parts of the brain by removing parts and observing the effects. Perhaps not surprisingly, he found that all functions grew

---

[2] It is suggested that humans are the only animals that think about their own thinking, or metacognition.

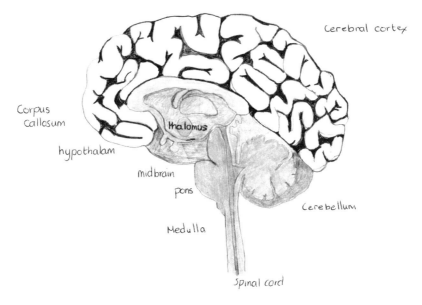

Figure 1.1 Structure of the brain

weaker as more and more of the brain was removed!

Although learning and memory are features of all of the brain, there are two elements that are seen to be in constant conversation with each other. The first is the thalamus, the oldest part of the brain, and the second is the cortex, the part of the brain only found in highly developed animals. The cortex increases in size with an increasing ability to 'learn'. There is evidence of a link between the thalamus and the cortex because 'Ping-Pong'-like electrical currents can be traced backwards and forwards between the two.

Whilst there is evidence that some parts of the brain have specific functions, Greenfield (1995: 22) believes that compartmentalising the brain leads to a focus on, 'the trees at the expense of the forest'. In other words, it is far more tempting to focus on the parts of the brain because this offers a neat and organised approach. It is tidy and comforting to think that a specific function happens in a set place, but taking such an approach and focusing on the different sections individually, ignores how they work together. As there is no specific part of the brain where memory or consciousness is found, it is more important to have an overall knowledge of the working of the brain than the function of each part if an understanding of learning is going to be developed.

In the same way that an understanding of the solar system developed as new information was gained, so understanding how the brain works

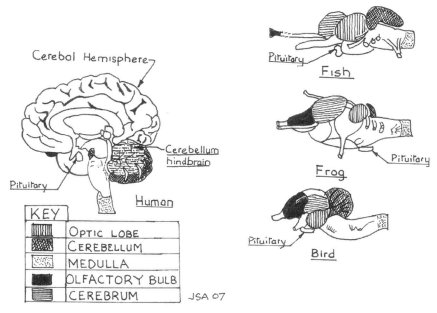

Figure 1.2 Comparing different animal brains
It can be seen that the human brain is more developed than those of other animals. The different regions work together to provide learning. Talking and language facilitate this.

has developed as more information has emerged. Developments in neuroscience have proved that not all the neurons in a particular region of the brain worked in the same way (Hubel and Wiesel, 1962). Some cells were found to be rather fussy about what 'got them going'. The chemicals were present and the electrical impulses, but some neurons did not get excited. This led to a suggestion that although neurons linked together and passed chemicals and electricity, perhaps there could be a hierarchical system operating where some neurons further up the chain only noted specific events, such as the ability to recognise a specific person, for example, one's mother. Scientists now believe that rather than a hierarchy in which specific cells have a set function, a system exists instead where neurons work in parallel and that all neurons are capable of working in a variety of ways. This is a helpful way of looking at the brain as it suggests that neurons are active all the time and can be used in many ways, rather than lying dormant until, for instance, your mother appears.

There are more than 50 different types of neurons that have different shapes as well as sizes. Neurons also have many functions and can therefore be involved in many different activities. Greenfield (1995) used an analogy of the roles people have in life – for example, teacher, parent, daughter, member of a sports team or club, aunt, niece, soprano in a choir. In the same way, neurons are able to undertake many tasks and this enables learning to take place throughout a person's life without the brain running out of neurons. So although humans have fewer neurons than an octopus, they use the ones they have much more effectively. Such a complex network also allows for communication between neurons and therefore links can be made. Furthermore, when these links are established learning takes place.

In the cortex it is thought that there are ten billion neurons that connect to each other in one million billion ways. The permutation for how these neurons can connect is more than the total number of positively charged particles in the known universe. Neurons do not all link together in a set way; it depends on the stimuli as to how they react. Behaviourists believe that stimuli affect response, as in the case of Pavlov and his work with dogs. Pavlov trained a dog to expect food when a bell was rung. With training, the dog would salivate when the bell was rung even before the food appeared. Gestalt psychologists, however, believe it is the association with a response that will result in an action, that just ringing a bell and getting a response is too simplistic to explain how other functions link together. For example, in humans the food provided might suit one person but might not be liked by another.[3] The word 'Gestalt' means a unified or meaningful whole; thus the brain works as a whole and is more complex than a simple stimulus reaction model.

Simple stimulus response mechanisms work only for basic functions and not for systems as complex as learning. In addition to the stimulus, the response is also affected by and dependent upon prior experience. How the neurons react, how many of them work together, or whether they react at all, depends on what neurons have already been recruited to this stimulus and whether any other processing is happening at the same time. It is true that the more powerful the stimulus the greater the number of brain cells that are recruited, and as our environment is full of many stimuli happening concurrently, recruitment happens quickly. However, if too many stimuli are given then the starting chain does not have time to grow before another chain of neurons replaces it. Greenfield pictured these chains as epicentres, as with earthquakes, and named them gestalts.

---

[3] Which is why one behaviour system will not work with all learners, as they might not be influenced by stimuli in the same way as other learners.

> The triggering of associations is analogous to rain drops hitting the surface of a puddle and creating ever widening concentric ripples. (Greenfield, 1995: 91)

Every day the human body is bombarded by stimuli and is likely to have a continuum of arousal. If there are too many reactions to the stimuli then each epicentre will be replaced by a new one before it can grow. Conversely, if there is too little arousal the recruiting power of the epicentre is too low to have impact. The most efficient epicentres will be those that have time to grow and develop like 'the raindrop in the puddle'. Therefore bigger gestalts will recruit many neurons, whilst small gestalts will have fewer neurons and last for less time.

Hebb (1949) suggested that the more neurons are linked with each other the easier communication becomes. This has an implication for teaching as it suggests that activities that promote communication between neurons will make thinking easier. Some current researchers have suggested that the brain is like any muscle and needs to be exercised in order to gain in size and potential (see Kawashima, 2007). Certainly research with rats has shown that their brains grow the more they are exercised and that through greater challenges the rats were able to transfer learning into new settings (Greenough and Bailey, 1988).

Neurons linking

It has been found that it is not only the way neurons link to each other but also the strength of the signal that impacts on what is perceived. In the First World War, it was noted that soldiers who had lost their sight could still reach out for objects that were in motion and often thought when they caught them that it had been by accident. However, the regularity with which they were able to reach out and grab the moving objects was too high for this to be mere chance. In addition, the faster the objects moved or the brighter the light, the greater the soldiers' reactions. Because they were blind they were not aware of seeing the objects or sensing them as a sighted person might, however the brain was sensing and acting upon the stimuli and the greater the stimuli the more positive the effect. The research was developed further and one of the key features that emerged in improving the soldiers' ability to catch an object was the effect caused by the act of guessing. The process of guessing causes more neurons to work together, giving a greater signal. Guessing, therefore, is an important way to help the brain to make links. Although not developed from a neuroscience approach, Bruner (1960) suggested also that learners should be given training in recognising the plausibility of guessing. Educated guesses should be encouraged and do aid learning.

How do we know the neurons link together as gestalts?

Evidence for the links between neurons working as gestalts, or like raindrops on puddles, comes from a number of sources. One of these is through recording images of the brain whilst a person sleeps. When asleep and in a dreaming stage (known as rapid eye movement or REM), there is evidence of some electrical activity though this is less than when a person is awake. The neurons make links with each other and epicentres are created. When dreaming there are many small epicentres that are not strong enough to grow, and as a result pictures, memories and events swirl through a person's unconsciousness. In dreamless sleep, which is often called deep sleep, there is little electrical activity. It is far harder to wake from REM sleep than in those periods when little electrical activity is occurring, as the neurons are already reacting to events 'within the dream'. It takes more stimuli to recruit neurons to the sound of an alarm clock than if a person is in a deep sleep where there is little competition for the neurons. Periods of dreamless sleep are vital as these provide time to enable the brain to grow.

The links and concentric spread of neuron activity, or the gestalt, are affected by the genetic make-up of a person as well as the impact of the environment on that person. Also of importance are those happenings which the brain has already reacted to, namely prior experience. It is suggested that as the neurons are recruited to the gestalt this recruitment is individualised, as particular groups of neurons are selected out of the billions of possibilities. Whilst babies have brains that have few opportunities to make links, the associations accrue as children grow and as events and stimuli take on significance. Information processing develops with increasing age. It is thought that one year-old children can process one item of information at a time and this increases to three pieces of information by the time they reach the age of five. By the age of 11 children may be able to process four pieces of information. Adults do not necessarily process more but can do so faster, therefore getting through more information (Newton, 1996). If associations are made regularly then the same neurons are recruited and the links become stronger. This is called Hebbran Strengthening.

Hebbran Strengthening of the neuronal contacts is thought to enable learning (Freeman, 1991). It was Hebb in the 1940s who first suggested that neurons work together in what he called an 'assembly' and that these assemblies were strengthened by experience. He pictured this process as making pathways in the brain between neurons situated in the different parts. The pathways worked together with different assemblies at different times. This is also sometimes called 'hard wiring', where more permanent pathways or groupings of neurons are made. If a stimulus recruits neurons to the gestalt and this stimulus is repeated again and again, the links between these neurons become stronger. Examples of this include learning the times tables or riding a bike. Even if the pathway is not used for a while, it can easily be recalled into action.

Creativity and new thought

The theory that neurons start from an epicentre and grow outwards is clear and has been supported by evidence (Greenfield, 1995). When two competing epicentres occur at the same time it is possible for there to be a shift in focus from one centre to another. If there is increasing sensitivity to something new then a new epicentre will occur. It is also possible that the epicentre will not be related to an outside stimulus. This could result in brain activity that is not linked to reality. Generally though, this new gestalt can result in a new thought, a new idea or a new way of linking ideas together. Humans are the only animals that have metacognition, which is the ability to think about the thinking process. Each brain area works as a coordinated whole and the size of the gestalt is linked to the size of the activity. Children can form only small gestalts as they are still developing their ability to link neurons together. For them their days are filled with many small gestalts and it is not surprising that for a child time seems to go on forever. Many adults remember when it seemed to take an eternity to get to Christmas, yet as age increases, time seems to speed up. This is related to the way in which the gestalts are formed and their size. Adults with brain damage who are not able to develop large gestalts also suffer from dragging time, and are not able to settle to anything. Some conditions that inhibit the brain from reacting to outside stimuli result in an inability to develop competing gestalts. This results in patients who are seemingly catatonic. Whilst small gestalts occur in dream sleep as well as in childhood, large gestalts are formed in adults particularly when they are focused on demanding or enjoyable activities and time just seems to fly. Yet even adults can have periods when time seems to have stopped; for example, when waiting for an important phone call everything else becomes irrelevant and time drags interminably as no other gestalts can form.

Implications of gestalts for teaching and understanding

In order to be effective the brain needs to make these links termed gestalts. The relevance of this learning or knowledge will affect whether a network of understanding is developed. Learners can experience difficulty in learning if simple tasks are made too complex. This is because the system becomes overloaded. Ensuring clear effective links are made is the role of the teacher. Teachers with good subject knowledge are able to think logically through a pathway and make clear the links between each piece of information. This in turn helps learners to make necessary associations. Some children have problems in understanding the relevance of some science lessons because they have little relevance to previous lessons and there is meagre opportunity to develop the links and pathways. This is also true of some published schemes of work.

The brain can be bombarded by stimuli and small gestalts result. This is short-term memory. In order to be effective the information being delivered must be understood, and this relies on the brain making links with what is already known. This is termed long-term memory or prior knowledge and is important if learning is to take place. If the mental models held in the long-term store are faulty then this will impact on future learning. If this is a new area of experience for the learner, then there will be no prior knowledge with which to link the new information. New links (assemblies of neurons) have to be made. If prior knowledge exists then it can enable sense to be made of the information gathered; this in turn will make the pathways stronger and the learning more likely to be retained.

'Chunking' is an important aspect of learning and improves the brain's ability to make sense of information because similar pieces of information are linked together. It is thought that this works by helping learners to make associations of new learning with a pathway that is already there. If prior knowledge is accessed, pathways already present are used and can help develop greater pathways. Deciding how to use prior knowledge and how to make links is important and sometimes teachers, who have a greater personal knowledge of science, can forget what it was like not to know. They may then try to provide learners with answers in a way that confuses them and overloads the system with too much, too fast.

In fact, as humans age they are more likely to have prior knowledge to draw upon and be able to use associations and chunking to free up their own mental space. The learners they work with will not have such a range of connections, and so from a science perspective the amount of information given to learners should be relative to their age and therefore much less for younger children. Even with older learners it is important to ensure that each explanation builds on prior knowledge and therefore makes sense to the learner. Whilst it is clear that human brains are immensely clever and have almost limitless power, they are not the same as computers and should not be treated as if they were.

The brain as a computer

It is often suggested that the human brain is like a computer and is programmable in the same way. If this were true it would make teaching and learning much easier than they really are. However, research suggests that the analogy of the brain as a computer is unhelpful and inaccurate. Computers work in a digital way. They are either 'on' or 'off'. However, in the brain the neurons work in a more gradual manner and in fact some respond to chemicals by becoming sensitive but also by exhibiting no immediate change. At a later time this sensitivity will result in a greater output in response to an insignificant input, which is called 'priming' or 'conditioning'. Computers have memory cards that can be called into play. Here the memory is of a fixed size and it is found in a set place. Greater memory in a computer can be added by installing additional cards but the human brain does not have such devices and memory is not stored in one place. The many different types of neurons with varying shapes and sizes behave in different ways, again makes the brain different from a computer or its software.

Another difference between the workings of the brain and a computer relates to feelings. Sometimes things happen or are registered as a result of human feelings or actions, for example, in going for a walk or watching a sunset. The ways humans function do not always have a specific purpose and sometimes there are things that occur and are registered for seemingly no particular reason. This apparent lack of reason is a central factor when considering learning and it is essential to provide provision for differing ways of working.

Learners do not have brains like computers so it is not helpful to turn out mechanical and robotic learners. Future societies will be more grateful if learners are able to make links through thoughts and ideas and to see things in different ways. They will then be able to continue to adapt to the changing needs of the environment and the world in which they live and for which they have responsibility. Human brains are linked and wired in order for this to happen and teaching should thus provide the relevant stimuli, desires and opportunities.

Issues with computers and learning

With the advent of the computer and the internet age human memory may no longer be as essential as it was in the past, for example, in remembering such things as key historical dates (such as the Battle of Hastings or the Great Fire of London). Furthermore, whilst this may be seen as a good thing, the increase in computer use among learners might not always be seen as an equally good thing when considering the development and use of the brain. In fact, Greenfield (2006: 2) considers this in relation to all humans.

> Along with the ability to read and the need to remember, surely we are at risk of losing our imagination, that mysterious and special cognitive achievement that until now has always made the book so very much better than the film.

Clearly there is concern about the impact on children's imagination but there is also concern over the increasing numbers of children with hyperactivity. There is some thought that this might be explained by sustained exposure to an unsupervised IT environment, where only short attention spans are needed and where a child has no way of practising long periods of paying attention. Greenfield (2006) suggests that whilst this is a speculative idea it should be at least tested. Surveys suggest that the average child is spending about six and a half hours a day using electronic media, and if the trend to multi-tasking (using more than one device at a time) is taken into account, this average rises to more than eight hours a day. This could have lasting implications for the way in which the brain works, and how links and pathways are made. Using technology to support learning is important, but it should be adopted to meet the needs of the learner and not to have the learner change to suit the technology.

Summary

The brain is a muscle and can be developed. It is composed of cells called neurons. It is not the number of neurons that is important but the way in which they link together. Although there are different parts of the brain, most important functions take place throughout it. Therefore focusing on parts of the brain is less effective than seeing the functioning of the whole. The brain works by responding to a number of stimuli and it is not a simple reaction response system, rather it works as a united whole. The neurons work by making links with each other and these links spread outwards like a series of ripples across a pond. These 'ripples' are called gestalts.

   Learning develops the links in the brain and these links are developed into pathways. Some links are used so often they are said to be 'hardwired', but hardwiring might not make links that can be used in new settings. Rote learning promotes hardwiring but does not always promote understanding. Having an understanding of how the brain works can help with the development of suitable learning methods. These are discussed in the next chapter on learning, memory and motivation.

Putting this into practice
- In order for the complex networks between neurons to be effective, provide learning in a number of ways to help maximise the links.
- As the brain is more complex than a simple input–stimuli–output system, behaviour responses are limited. Providing opportunities to personalise the learning for all age groups is vital.
- Guessing should be encouraged and learners should be helped to provide a range of ideas of what they think, and not just focus on one prediction.
- Make tasks simple and ensure lessons build on each other. Making it simple is not the same as doing learning for the learner; independence should always be fostered.
- Emotions affect learning; time spent encouraging positive feelings towards the subject is worthwhile.

2

Learning, memory and motivation

This chapter will explore how learners can be involved with learning. Without self-belief and an awareness of their strengths, and some control over their learning, then real and lasting achievement is not possible. Teachers will recognise what children knew the year before but have subsequently forgotten. Memory – what it is, how it works, and how to use it effectively – will be explored here, as well as the teachers' role in helping to enable transferable learning. In order for learning to be effective, learners need to be involved in the whole process, including in any decisions about planning and assessment. Russell and McGuigan (2003) indicate that little can be truly learnt by rote, and what is tends to be trivial if not applied. Therefore learning science should be more than a series of facts and a focus on external testing.

Learning

It would be very useful and helpful if everything that was taught was learnt. However, learners do not learn everything that has been taught and they will always omit or misinterpret some of it. This would not be too problematic if at the same time they were not just as likely to learn something totally different, inadequate and occasionally even contrary to what was intended. Learning can be defined in many ways but here it is regarded as the process that results in relatively lasting changes in mental capacity, motor skills, emotional wellbeing, motivation, social skills, attitudes and/or cognitive structure. Cognitive structure is hard to measure as increases in brain cells are not easy to judge, but as the brain is built of muscle it can be made, like all muscles, to work better, more effectively and to generate more links and assemblies.

Learning can occur throughout life and it is often suggested that children learn more in pre-school than at any later stage. Whilst it is true that children's brains grow faster at this time, some of this growth is due to the requirements of a smaller brain at birth. The brain has developed throughout the evolutionary past of the human race and has adapted to ensure that our species survives into the future. To be an effective learner requires flexibility, creativity, initiative and to have a sense of worth. The problem is that these are all attributes that have previously been thought to be part of a learner's personality. Building Learning Power teaching activities have been developed to focus upon these traits (Claxton, 2002). These activities teach metacognition and problem solving which are vital for increasing links in learners' brains.

In the early stages of development children learn by watching and mimicking adults and others. This is called cumulative learning (Nissen, 1970). Babies will not understand the process of dissolving or how to work out line-graphs – partly because they lack the learning prerequisite but mainly because they have a largely undifferentiated central nervous system. The advantage of cumulative learning is that it does not have to link to any other learning, which is useful as there is little there to begin with for it to utilise. What is there has been pre-wired and, in the first months and years, areas of the brain are ready to receive information from the senses; notably for children to learn language, to sense the environment, to hear and to see. If some of these areas of the brain are not used, other sensors will quickly use them. So children who have sight defects that are not picked up in the first few months may find they are sight-reduced for the rest of their lives, as these areas of the brain are used by other senses instead, often for hearing sound. However, the majority of the brain is very plastic in nature and it can readapt many areas if they receive damage at an early age.

Motivation

One person cannot directly motivate others; motivation comes from within. (Biehler and Snowman, 2000: 122)

Learning is affected by whether or not a learner thinks they are clever, as well as by how effective a teacher is at making links. There are also social and emotional aspects of learning which will impact on whether what is happening in the taught part of the lesson has relevance for that learner. Incidents that happened outside the classroom and whether the learner feels emotionally able to focus on generating meaning also affect learning. The brain can be tied up with gestalts concerned with other elements of a learner's life, leaving little time for making cognitive links. In addition, learners can think they are smart or not smart and will thus give themselves a label or will be labelled by others. Many five year-olds know whether they are in the top, middle or bottom group.

> *We are writing two sentence, we are the top group.* (Five year-old boy)

Being identified as such at an early age can be problematic both for the 'gifted' who worry about staying gifted, and also for the 'less gifted', who feel they have no worth. Dweck (one of the key writers on motivation and learning) suggests that teachers should encourage children to see learning as something everyone can do:

> to value learning over the appearance of smartness, to relish challenge and effort, and to use errors as routes to mastery. (Dweck, 1999: 4).

If only a few learners can achieve and be top of the class then the focus will be on safety and not on growth. It is important to diminish physiological problems including the risk of failing and to know instead that risk taking is acceptable. In science the targets should be learner-centred and focused so that they are challenging but achievable. For example:

> Last time we played Kim's game you remembered seven items. See if you can beat that score today.

> Or

> Last time the class played a science link it took three minutes to answer all the questions. Shall we try for less than three minutes today?

It is important to comment upon the positive, to help re-order a learner's personal view of themselves as a learner. It is known that learners with low self-esteem see their failures as being due to their lack of ability, whilst high achievers sometimes think of any problems as being related to a lack of effort on their part. It is possible that the way the praise is given might reinforce the learner's viewpoint. Teachers who have all learners working to the best of their ability use the spontaneous expression of admiration and praise (for example, '*Wow, what a great explanation*') along with the view that they already thought the learner would succeed (such as, '*I knew you could do this!*'). They also make links between one success and the next step ('*Now you can make a series of measurements, it will be easier to explain these at the end*'). Effective teachers also give encouragement and even when the task was difficult for learners they will comment on how they kept going and did not give up. Effective teachers do not pretend to learners that learning is easy! Teachers who make learning more difficult can interrupt the learning without realising, and usually just as learners need to be focused on the task. Such teachers keep flipping from one thing to another, interrupting to comment on something that is irrelevant or on trivial things, like a dropped jumper, all of which interrupt thinking and thought patterns.

Why things are not learnt

There are a number of reasons why not all the things that are taught are likely to be learnt. Jarvis (1992) thought non-learning could be divided into three reasons

- **Presumptions** Here the learner already thinks they know it (even if they do not) and therefore do not see new learning possibilities. This is often found when a topic in science is reintroduced and learners say they have done this before. Even though it was at a lower level, topics like electricity are prone to such reactions.
- **Non-considerations** Here there are areas of new things to learn but learners are too busy or too nervous to become involved. This happens sometimes in science when the scheme of work does not have enough links between activities and so every session does not have a clear link to the previous one. This can affect less able learners most and the result can be that everything seems too much and every lesson is something new.
- **Rejection** Here learners make the conscious decision not to get involved. This happens when they think the subject is too hard, or they have feelings of inadequacy, or where the relationship with the teacher or peers means they do not want to be involved. This is more likely to be found with older learners who have already experienced failure or boredom.

In order to ensure that non-learning is reduced, it is vital to start every topic with a link that shows how it will develop what has been

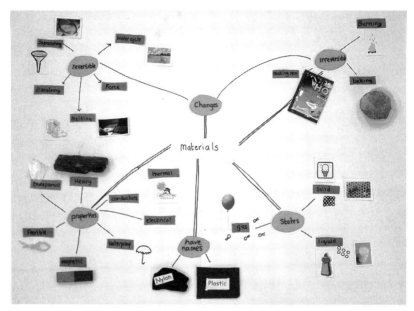

Figure 2.1 A visual map of learning
The map starts the process of what will be learnt in a topic of materials in Key
Stage 2. It can be added to throughout the topic and used later for revision.

learned before; this is where a visual map of learning is helpful.[1]

This will show how what was learnt before links to what will be learnt next, helping to reduce non-learning from presumptions. By ensuring that some time is spent building learners' self-esteem can reduce non-consideration. Science coordinators often report taking over new classes who 'Do not like science', but will then describe how the learners become motivated and enthused as they start undertaking more interesting types of science activities. Sometimes just placing learners in different groupings or involving them in a problem-solving or creative approach can be very effective, as there is no expectation of just one right answer. Using such approaches can reduce the chances of rejection as they promote a belief that all learners can be effective in science. By including a range of recording methods alongside short brain-favoured activities, such as class or team games/activities (for example, science bingo, 'What if?', or drama), can support all learners and reduce the occurrence of non-consideration and rejection.

---

[1] 'Students usually had a good understanding of what to do for individual tasks but were less clear as to how these tasks fitted into the 'big picture' of the course. There was evidence they were not always receiving the 'signposting' they needed'. (Weeden, Winter and Broadfoot, 2000: 2).

Here are some responses by learners to the question 'What words come to mind when you hear the word science?'[2]

Oh, no, great. Another boring lesson. I want to go home. (Boy, Year 5)

Well at first I think I don't want to do it, but then once I get used to it I get stuck in. (Girl, Year 5)

Oh no. Science is boring and it does not excite me. (Boy, Year 5)

Experiments and fun. (Girl, Year 5)

SATS. (Boy, Year 6)

Once attitudes have been improved, the focus is on how to make the learning 'stick'.

How memory works

Learners bridge the present and the future by using their memories of the past. (Curzon, 2000: 11)

One of the key questions concerning memory is, 'Why are some things easier to remember than others?' It would be helpful if all that was learned was permanently retained, but it is encouraging to know that there can be no learning without an element of memory, as patients with brain damage have shown. In the same way that teaching and learning (although talked about together) are not the same thing, memory and learning are not always related. Whilst the memory might be a bridge over the flow of time, it is both more and less than an inner record of all a person has lived through (Doyle, 1987). It is 'more', in that the brain can add to information by creating new memories, sometimes of things that really did not happen, and also 'less', as some of the inputs experienced are not stored and are 'lost' forever.

Using a model of memory in three stages can help to develop teaching strategies that make the most of what is taught. Starting the process off requires 'registration'. Registration is where the brain is stimulated and this stimulus is encoded, or acknowledged by the brain. The information is then stored using a process called 'retention'. The final stage is 'retrieval', where the information is used again. However, while this stage is called 'retrieval', the information/memory/learning is not really retrieved but reconstructed. The memory is not sitting there waiting to be picked up, like a fish on the end of a line.

---

[2] The responses are from a larger questionnaire looking at children's attitudes to science; all these learners were in different schools (Ward, unpublished).

Short- (primary) term and long- (secondary) term storage exist and it is known that the short-term or working memory has a limited capacity. The short-term memory consists of things that are still in a person's consciousness, whilst the long-term memory is for non-conscious thoughts. There are many different types of memories that are stored long term: personal or episodic memories; semantic memories containing facts and general knowledge; procedural memories which are those concerned with skills. Although it would be easy to centre understanding only on those that focus on facts and skills, episodic memories are images stored from the past and are therefore important. Children not only know less than adults because of their lack of experience, they also need help with knowing what to do with what they know (Fisher, 1990: 96).

The first place to start in helping to promote memories that last is with registration. The more attention that is given to the details of the stimuli, the more likely a learner is to remember that stimuli and the associated learning. Ideas need to be introduced using a number of stimuli. If concepts in science are just spoken about there is little to alert the brain that this bit is important because there are too few stimuli. Starting with pictures that link to scientific vocabulary provides more than one stimuli. This is helpful because it is known that the brain has a larger capacity for pictures than words. Showing children pictures of rainproof materials, together the word 'waterproof', improves registration and can help learners to make associations that can support learning. Using a thought-provoking starter question can make learners think. So when beginning a topic on materials and their properties, a simple but thought-provoking starter of 'How many things could you use a blanket for?' will focus attention on what materials are used for. There is no set answer here and the learners can make links to many aspects that will help registration.

If the registration is strong enough then it might develop something called 'spotlight memories'. These are clear because of the focus on a real event as opposed to abstract memories. While spotlight memories can be defined as the rounded experience of tasting wine, other memories can be delightfully defined as the dregs at the bottom of the bottle, stripped down to the bare elements. The first is so much more effective and enjoyable than the second! However, while science lessons cannot be filled with only spotlight memories, a few more than are commonly found would not be harmful. Spotlight memories do not equate to understanding, for example, a spotlight memory from my childhood which involved seeing a banana being frozen in liquid nitrogen – which shattered when struck against a science bench. I did not understand the science fully until much later but I can still picture the event in great detail.

These two major retention systems are of different sizes and short-term memory can be very easily overloaded. When this happens a choice has to be made – what to keep and what to let go. Learners often remember the first and last thing in a lesson and most learners are influenced by the 'seven plus or minus two' rule (Miller, 1956). This rule is helpful as it suggests that generally only seven (plus or minus two) pieces of information will be retained by learners. This means that not only does the information need to have a high stimulus at registration, it also needs to be limited in amount. Johnson (1984) demonstrated that a learner's ability to solve problems decreased as the number of pieces of information increased. The impact on what, and how much, can be kept is also dependant on the types of information provided. For example, there is less room for longer words than shorter ones and if the information has a resonance with a learner it has more likelihood of being retained as it makes sense. The more tired learners are, or the more abstract and unusual the information provided, the lower the chances of registration and retention. If 20 points are made, only six might make it into the long-term memory. And the choice of the six is down to the individual!

Games provide useful ways to improve retention as they have high registration features and the repetition of playing improves both retention and retrieval. 'Kim's game' is excellent for improving memory, thinking and gaining an understanding of equipment. Provide a tray on which the science equipment to be used in the topic is displayed. (The fun element of this makes it likely to be registered, because it is something different.) Name each object, in turn, and then show them all for a further minute. Cover them and ask the learners to remember as many as they can. Teams or mixed ability groups can be helpful and the game is fun to play in pairs.

Other ways to improve retention and retrieval are

- **Science word memory** Start with five words for young learners and stretch to ten for older or experienced players. Number the words, for example (1) stem, (2) root, (3) leaf, (4) flower, (5) petal (younger learners) and ask them to remember what was number 4? And then number 2? With older learners the words and their quantity can be increased, for example (1) root, (2) stem, (3) stamen, (4) style, (5) flower, (6) stigma, (7) ovule, (8) ovary, (9) leaf, (10) sepal. Questions such as, 'What is at number 5?' or even 'Which number is ovule?' can be increased to include, 'Who can give the name of the plant which is two more than stamen?' This game takes only a few minutes and can be changed for different parts of the science curriculum. It also helps with retention as the more reminding the brain gets, the better it is at recall, so repetition, as long as it does not become boring or pressuring, is recommended.

- **Word associations** Show a picture and the names of two objects and ask learners to see if they can make a link between these. These can be given by the teacher or by a child. Recently, a child suggested 'apple' and 'computer' and the class were able to make a number of links, first was the name of a computer (Apple) and then that they both have important things inside, and that both are smooth on the outside and opaque, etc. Making links between objects and how they are alike helps with the development of analogy, a useful skill in science.

- **Science suitcase** As the science topic progresses key pieces of information, objects or equipment should be placed into the science suitcase. At the start of each lesson, learners should be asked what is in the suitcase and to talk to each other about what was saved and why. For example in a topic on electricity, in the first lesson there might be a battery-operated toy that works by having the electrical terminals joined,[3] a battery, a bulb and a flash card saying complete circuit. In the next lesson additional components like buzzers can be added, or pictures of electricity in real life, or of work completed in the lesson. A total of about four things per lesson seems to work well. This also helps learners to make associations between items.

The ability to link ideas together and make meaning develops with age. At the age of two children can relate only two items of information. This rises to four in most adults, although the speed of dealing with this information also increases with age (Halford, 1993). In order to be successful in science learners require the ability to link ideas and develop meaning. However, overloading small brains is never successful.

Strategies to help retrieval

There are many reasons why retrieval fails. This may be temporary, for example when calling people by the wrong name, or it can be

---

[3] Ghost balls (www.tobar.co.uk) or a plastic light-up duck or chirping chicken can be used. Place the learners in a circuit and get them to hold hands with the toy placed between two of them, each using one finger on each terminal to complete the circuit. When all hands are held the electricity will flow, if a break in the circuit occurs, by a hand not being held, the toy will not work.

where things are not retrieved on purpose, such as an unpleasant experience that is best forgotten. Retrieval is less effective where the materials introduced at the beginning of a session or topic have no link to any previous learning. If the teacher can link new materials to things that are already known, the learning will make greater sense. If it makes sense this will involve neuron assemblies, some of which have already been linked (as explained in Chapter 1). This means a learner is more prepared to receive the information, as the *registration* is not of something totally new. This is where teaching skills are important in showing the relevance of what is being taught and in helping to arouse interest and maintain involvement in the topic by learners. The learning has to make sense to learners, so they should be encouraged to record their experiences in their own words or through other methods. (This is developed later in Chapter 5.)

Retrieval also fails if the knowledge is not used, as it will lose the associated memory traces thus making the knowledge obsolete. Repetition is helpful and should be undertaken in ways that develop learning into new settings. Helping learners to organise information into chunks will also help with retrieval, and the use of mnemonics[4] such as MRS-GREN (movement, respiration, sensitivity, growth, reproduction, excretion and nutrition) can help children to remember the seven processes of life. However, the use of mnemonics is only helpful when these can be remembered, and if left unused it too will be forgotten. This is called 'cue dependent forgetting'. Much of secondary science falls into this category for most members of the public.

Another way of helping with organisation is by putting large amounts of information into smaller chunks and singing it. The vital point here is that the songs not only have to scan but also should be scientifically correct! The following is sung to the tune of 'Frère Jacques' and contains a common misconception (as heat will pass through insulators but very slowly). Songs are most effective when they provide a sound basis and also contain information chunked up in a way that is easier to remember. A song is less useful if the information within it is not really worth singing about!

Thermal insulation	*Covers and gloves*
Thermal insulation	*Covers and gloves*
Hot water bottles	*Heat won't pass*
Hot water bottles	*Heat won't pass*

---

[4] *Mnasthai*, to remember in Greek

Memory loss

The greatest loss of knowledge happens quickly after the input and then memory loss slows down. However, the passing of time provides opportunities for interference with these memories, which also contributes to lack of retrieval. In a way this makes it appear as if the memories are stored somewhere, like photographs in a box, but as stated in Chapter 1, memory is not located in one area, it is the firing of neurons that supports understanding and memories are not in a filing system. Cue dependent forgetting happens because the cues present at the time of learning are not present at the time of recall. This is a key problem for those isolated pieces of knowledge or memories from childhood. The stimulus that starts the chain of events is missing so there is nothing to get a gestalt started.

Early memories of childhood classrooms will flood back to teacher training students when they sit on those small chairs and are immersed in the environment of their younger days after an absence of more than a decade. Sometimes the cue is provided by sitting at that low level, although many report that the thing they were most aware of as other memories came flooding back was the 'smell of school'! Learners who sit tests or exams in a hall or gymnasium are robbed of cue dependant factors that would be present in their classrooms. Even when posters or displays are removed, the eyes will travel to where they were previously and the brain will picture the materials and their content.

Changing the context

If the learning involves materials that are very similar then there is a higher rate of memory loss. A clear example of this was seen in the science National Test for eleven year-olds in 2006 (see Chapter 7). The children seemed to have problems selecting the type of equipment to use to separate mixtures of materials such as sand, gravel and salt, with a number of inaccurate suggestions for separating salt and water which included 'scoop it out with a spoon'. These activities are often taught in one small section of a scheme of work and developed together in a short time frame. As a result children may not have enough time and space to think about the process of dissolving or separating insoluble mixtures with filter paper and funnel or sieve. Some teachers also think that filtering and sieving are simple and straightforward and that learners understand them after using the equipment only a few times. This approach suggests a model of knowledge being put into learners' heads in the manner of filling a sieve full of sand. Over time the sand falls through the holes and is left behind, in the classroom and on the corridor floor. By the end of the day very little of what was put in the sieve is still there. In each lesson more sand is added to the sieve; if it is similar it will be mixed together yet the stimulus may not be great enough for it to make it to the long term or secondary memory store.

Contrary to popular belief, memory is enhanced by being disturbed because the memory traces are thought to be active for longer than for those where tasks are completed (Zeigarnik, 1967).[5] However, classroom practice does not mirror this and it has become increasingly important to complete lessons in one sitting. This does demonstrate how well planned and in control teachers are generally. The focus is on teaching rather than learning. Organising learning to enhance memory traces requires detailed planning and decisions need to be made as to how the lesson or series of lessons should flow, which parts need to be re-emphasised and which elements will be introduced in one lesson and then revisited at a later date. Although this planning takes time it is worthwhile, especially for science, to ensure that the key aspects are revisited and investigations are used to support learning. Thus the whole process will have an impact on memory retention and retrieval.

Whilst planning it is important to ensure subjects that are similar in method or content will be separated by time. This in turn has implications for the structure of lessons and although it can be considered a strength of some systems, lessons with an introduction followed by a practical and then a plenary are just too similar. Therefore, the content becomes forgettable and likely to sink without trace. Varied lesson structures, time and content will impact on learners. In addition, once covered much of science is not revisited in a way that consolidates learning. Ludwig (1979) found that retention was doubled where the content of the lesson was repeated three weeks later.

Once ideas have been introduced using them in a new setting will help retention and retrieval. For example, after learners have had some experience of separating materials they should then be given different materials to do the same with, such as fools' gold, caster sugar, gemstones, two pence pieces from different times[6] and small crystals. They

---

[5] The Zeigarnik Effect: experiments by Bluma Zeigarnik showed that people remember interrupted tasks best. The reason for this is that the tension created by unfinished tasks helps memory. Zeigarnik worked with Vygotsky and her work was started after watching the way waiters remembered food orders.

[6] Two pence pieces minted after 1992 are magnetic, whilst those minted between 1971 and 1992 are not. The change was as a result of increases in the world's metal prices. The newer two pence coins have a steel centre, whilst the original ones were 97 per cent copper.

should also be encouraged to think about what they will do before doing it and to record their plan as a series of pictures. (It was the Greeks who suggested that imagery was an effective aid to memory.) Annotated diagrams are underused and can aid memory development. Some learners may initially need to be helped to use pictures in this way. One useful method is to enable learners to think of sequences in science as a mental walk, for example planning out the stages needed to separate mixtures, or drawing the stages in the life cycle of a plant.

Chunking to support memory and learning

In order for learning to make better sense, the link between the ideas taught needs to be clear and the teacher needs to think how science concepts fit together. Working out a concept chain can help with this. A concept chain for electricity is provided in Figure 2.2; it is at a higher level than necessary for teaching primary-aged children, but shows how the ideas can be linked.

The main concept of the subject should be taught first, and the less inclusive but more specific aspects should be taught later. This in some ways relates to the big ideas in science and provides a hook for future learning. In the same way as coats in a school classroom always fall onto the floor as they are piled on one hook, learning that is linked in only one way can be difficult to locate. Concepts therefore must not be taught in isolation and a visual framework should be provided as it is vital to show how concepts are related to each other. It is also helpful if things that are introduced at the start of a unit of work are then referred to again throughout a topic, so they are not merely introduced and then lost to future learning. This is where the science suitcase alongside the visual map helps. It is also helpful to use key words, sometimes called 'Peg' words, that are referred to in every lesson; reinforcement of a few words will help learners develop their understanding. (This is examined further in Chapter 5.)

How the materials are presented is important and the more logical the sequence that is provided the greater the chance of the material being remembered. Chunking the things that are alike together also aids learner memory. It is also noteworthy if learning is not merely superficial but is focused on deeper learning. Only deeper learning that is aimed at an understanding of the fundamental principles facilitates retention. What is required is meaningful learning and this is all about acquiring new knowledge and creating meanings that can be used in a number of settings. Rote learning does not require an under-

---

An electricity chain

Discovery of the phenomenon of static electricity.

Historical experience that led to the idea of + and - charge.

Cells to current electricity.

Development of cells, the work of Volta.

How cells work and why emf is used as a term for 'voltage' or pd even though it is not quite accurate.

Cells in series produce a larger voltage and cells in parallel are able to provide more current. Because in multiple parallel circuits a single cell may physically not be able to provide enough electrons quickly enough.

Cells lead to moving charge in conductors, current, electricity.

Definition of current (Amp = Coulombs/Second).

Understanding of how electrons carry current in a conductor because of delocalised electrons in a metal.

Must have a complete circuit.

All electrons move effectively instantaneously.

Resistance and its part in limiting the flow of electrons (giving effects such as heat and light).

Ideas of voltage: The higher the voltage the greater the energy available to the individual electrons and so the force that helps the electron to move round the circuit is greater, so they will try to move faster which produces greater current.

Buying electricity as energy, which is the work that the generator has to do in order to move electrons round the circuits that we use.

The electricity company finds it easier to measure the 'power' (WATTS) that we use and how long we use them for so we have bills measured in kWhr (1kWhr =3 600 000 J).

How to work out the power of an appliance (Power = Voltage x Current).

Importance of fuses to limit current (safety otherwise the wires will melt!).

Figure 2.2 A concept chain for electricity[7]

standing of the material, and cannot be effectively transferred as it requires a context.

Learning through doing

Science is often thought to be about learning through doing and that practical 'hands-on' science is the way that learners will learn. Whilst this approach does contain some truth, it is problematic on a number of levels. If the activity is interesting enough there will be an increase at registration, but the retention and retrieval will depend on how the activity is understood.

---

[7] With thanks to Bill Philips who made suggestions for this area.

Picture the following activity. A group of eight year-olds is adding bicarbonate of soda to vinegar and seeing the effect. It fizzes and goes all over the place; there is a high level of excitement and noise. This activity should make it into the memory. However, the problem is that it might not be retrieved if the meaning behind it is not understood, rather like the spotlight memory of the banana in liquid nitrogen introduced earlier. If asked about what happened with the liquid nitrogen and the banana the picture will be clear; if asked about states of matter and whether all things can be solid, liquid or gas, the banana will not register. In the same way the children will remember when they put bicarbonate of soda with vinegar and enjoyed the reaction, but many will not realise that this is a chemical change or what this meant.

This may be partly because they did not have the 'priming' of what a chemical change was and why it is important in science. In this case, when the children were tested later they did not make the link between this activity and chemical change.[8] But when they were asked, 'Do you remember when we put … ?', thus providing them with a cue, they did remember and were animated, however the fun activity on its own was not transferred to another setting.

Ausubel (1978) discussed learning as 'reception' or 'discovery'. With reception learning the learner is presented with the entire content of what is to be learnt in its final form. So using the bicarbonate example, the learners would have been told that there are two ways in which materials can change – one creates new things whilst in the other no new thing is created. Examples would be given from experiences learners had seen before. For example, there is no new material made when water changes from a solid to a liquid or even from a liquid to a gas. It looks different, but it is still water. Similarly, mixing sand and salt together does not result in anything new being formed and it is easy to get both substances back. Making new materials, however, results in changes that cannot easily be reversed. Learners are given a range of substances to add together and asked to decide if something new has been formed, whether it is a permanent change and what the evidence for their ideas is. The whole picture is given and learners then have to use examples to reinforce that learning.

---

[8] Sometimes the activity can be confused by additional information and as a result the children interpret the activity in a different way to that intended. Some other children mixed citric acid and bicarbonate together and enjoyed the reaction. The teacher told them that this is what makes the bubbles in lemonade. Later on a national test paper included a question using the same two substances, but the focus was on whether the material was a solid, liquid or gas. More than 60 per cent of the children labelled the solid mixture of citric acid and bicarbonate as a gas. I often wonder what the marker thought!

In 'discovery'[9] learning, learners have to discover for themselves the principle context before being able to add it to what is already known. The learners would get to look at the range of substances and add them together. They would see that some 'disappeared', some fizzed and some did nothing at all. They may be asked to record this in their books and to work out what was happening. In some cases the write-up happens later and is a class activity, which does not make links for most learners to the practical task carried out. This discovery approach is used partly because of the belief that if learners are told about the discovery beforehand it will give the game away, spoil their fun and make learning less effective. However, learners do not need to be told specifics just the key features of change. They will often need to have a mix of approaches and skilful questioning by teachers can help the process of reception.

CASE STUDY

'Is this magic or is it science?'[10]
A group of ten year-olds experienced a candle-burning activity using a mixture of reception, observation and teacher questioning. They did discover things but in a structured way.

The candles were in sand trays, long hair was tied back and groups of not more than six girls and boys were sat round a single candle. The teacher held on to the matches and lit and relit candles until the end, where the children, under supervision, undertook the lighting of the wax vapour. What follows are the stages in the lesson together with some of the key questions asked.

- Light the candles on each table and ask the children to talk about what is seen. Questions were asked about changes to the wick and the candle. Some observations were recorded on the board (activate prior knowledge).
- Focus questions were asked such as *'Is it the wick that burns? How do we know?'* (This helped to raise questions and challenge prior knowledge. The questions focused on common misconceptions held by many learners.)
- The teacher used a spent match to show that it is the candle wax that is burning not the wick. This was demonstrated by showing how a spent match will not relight until it is dipped in wax. When dipped it will burn. The teacher allowed more talking. *'Why did the match not burn again after it had burnt the first time?' 'What happened when it was put in the liquid wax? Why might that be?'* (Opportunities were provided for learners to share ideas and look for evidence.)

Continues overleaf

---

[9] H. Armstrong, one of the most famous science teachers, used the term 'discovery' but in fact his teaching methods involved reception and structured learning in chunks. His approach was new because students tried out the ideas practically; prior to this students learnt only from books.
[10] This approach also works with adults. Anne Goldsworthy (2006) demonstrated the use of reception and discovery with teachers at a science conference.

- Then the teacher moved on to the burning itself. Asking *'What does the candle need in order to burn?'* A glass jar was placed over the candle to show what happens when the air supply is stopped. (More talking and questioning followed on what could be happening and why.)
- Then the teacher relit the candles and let them burn for a while, asking the children *'What would happen if it were left to burn for five hours?'* (This activated previous experience and observations, helping the children to make links to what they already knew.)
- The teacher then blew out one candle but had a match ready to relight the white vapour. This showed the learners how it would relight even when the wick was not in the flame. Some time followed for experimentation with this property, but as only a few matches were in each box, this gave a clear end to the experimentation. Partners talked about what was happening and why: *'What is burning and what does that tell us?'* (Probing and attention-focused questions.)
- The teacher then placed a metal spoon near to the flame of one candle and left it for a few seconds. *'Look at the spoon. What can you see?'* *'Where did it come from?'* (More talk.) Then the teacher introduced science information about candles – carbon is formed when there is not enough oxygen to make the gas carbon dioxide. Information was provided but in small chunks (reception and then comprehension by questioning). Further questions were posed including *'Do you think anything else might be given off apart from the carbon?'*, *'Why could the carbon not be seen before the spoon was added?'*, *'Could this happen with other substances?'*
- The teacher relit the candles and then told one child on each table to place a jam jar over it but to allow air to circulate at the bottom. *'How has the glass changed?'* *'What can be seen?'*, *'What could this mist be?'* (More questions – attention-focused and application questions.)
- The teacher gathered all the ideas together and added the missing information that candles are hydrocarbons, that is they are made of carbon and hydrogen. (Reception and simple explanation.) The mist was water vapour condensing. Some children related this to mist on the mirror in a bathroom.
- The teacher then suggested that the children record a few words and a picture on relighting the candles under the question *'Is this magic or is it science?'*
- Later in the week the children undertook the drama of the candle (see page 69) to help reinforce this idea in another way.
- The following week the children planned and carried out an investigation on the question *'Will all candles burn as quickly?'*

Ideas here about burning were developed through this series of steps that took about 30 minutes. The children constructed their own ideas and talked, all of which enabled links to be made in the brain. No overload of information was given at any one time and there was an interplay between the talking and observation. From a brain perspective, the talking and observation work helped to make the links and keep the neurons firing. As information is built up it is managed effectively and more so than if instructions are all given at the start. Curiosity is maintained by the questions and challenges posed by the teacher,

Continues opposite

although this approach does require a good subject knowledge on the part of the teacher. The fire element makes registration likely but the reception input throughout helps learners understand what is going on. It is also clear from this example that more than three pieces of information is needed to be linked together in order for full understanding to occur, so this activity was suited to learners over the age of nine. Learners below this age are only just beginning to link three things together.

The right thing at the right time

Teaching the right thing at the right age has always caused issues in science. When is the right time and is primary science stealing all the good stuff from the secondary curriculum? For example, it is easy to give children prisms in Reception and for them to see that light can be changed into all the colours of the rainbow; the problems come when children are told that light is white light and made of different colours. Young, developing brains will not grasp this abstract idea. It is important that children gain as many early experiences and as much observation of the world around them as is possible. What is not needed at such an early age is an explanation of why everything works. If, once the observations are made, the teaching rushes head-long into explanations, the brain is not developed enough yet to make sense of the ideas. As a result understandings develop which work for the learner, but are often unscientific.

Young children should be given interesting things to observe and play with, but the focus should be on comparing and asking questions about what is happening and whether this will it happen with all materials. Looking for materials that make colours appear and those that do not – the focus should be on developing experience and vocabulary, not on explanations which are unlikely to be understood. Some things when provided too young will encourage presumptions, 'we did this before', which could be problematic for future learning.

True understanding is not about the regurgitation of facts, although there are outstanding feats of memory (for example, some children are able to recite the *Torah* word perfectly). This proves how powerful the brain can be if it is helped to 'learn'. In the past when there were few books storytellers were able to memorise a fable and tell it through the generations. It is likely that the basic story was the same but the words and structure changed slightly each time. In order to be effective storytellers needed to understand the basic structure of a

story (and maybe the moral behind it), but the telling relied on reconstruction rather than verbatim repetition.

The role of telling

Some things can be found by looking, some can be found by testing and
some come from using a book. This is often called the 'look, test, book'
idea of science teaching. At times though, the art of telling should be
added to this list. Teaching for understanding is not about only one
approach and at times there is a need for learners to be told key facts
which they would not be able to find out quickly enough for themselves. In the candles activity, the fact that candles are hydrocarbons is
not something that could be discovered by observation, although it
could be found by secondary research. This would be time consuming,
would break the flow and would interrupt the learning sequence. When
telling it is important to consider which pieces of information are better told, which can be built up from direct observation and which pieces
learners can find out later without it affecting the construction of meaning. Telling, for extended periods of time, will not motivate most learners and will not invite a range of neurons to the learning party.

  The stimulus needs to be changed and a range of stimuli used. 'Minds
on' as well as 'hands-on' activities are vital. Furthermore, providing
opportunities for learners to talk is more productive for constructing
meaning than extended exposition by a teacher. 'Teacher talk' in science
is often too long, but information given at the right time can make the
light go on! Sometimes a teacher will find a good explanation, often
short, containing analogies that help learners to develop an understanding of an area of knowledge. It meets the needs of learners, and it
works – so it is used on a regular basis. The explanation may be refined
and regenerated yearly, in the best storytelling tradition, but the moral
is understood and history will have shown that this way of delivering
this piece of information is effective. Such explanations work because
they place something new into what is already known; there are already
networks of understanding and the explanation completes the picture
for the learner. Eureka moments come when something falls into place
rather than when something totally new emerges from nowhere.

ICT A computer analogy

In some cases a learner is viewed as an information processor who
uses their sensory stimuli to detect changes in the environment and

reacts to these as a result of past programming. But unlike a computer, the human mind has the ability to react to feelings and opinions. Why humans decide to do one thing and not another is not always logical but it will be affected by motivation and self-esteem. In science the need to tolerate uncertainty, to put ideas together and wonder as much about why things did not work, is often more important than why something did work. Scientific discoveries in the past have occurred as a result of things not working in the way they were expected to. This is the danger of presenting all science to learners via

ICT the computer, as computers do not get it wrong! A computer is programmed to show the 'right' things but many of the programs available, although often bright and colourful and sometimes motivating, can make the learner a passive responder to illuminated messages that have little meaning or relevance outside the programme (Fisher, 2005: 198). Many stimulation programs are too limiting to really place the leaner at the heart of the process and enable them to express their ideas and thoughts. These programs are very popular; cars can be raced on different surfaces, chemicals can be added and the effects watched, some even have sound! But perhaps the most restrictive aspect of computer-aided science education is that there is limited opportunity for learners to be creative, to make mistakes and to learn from these, or to add their own ideas or develop the ideas of others.

ICT Although the computer, via the internet, offers many possibilities to exchange information, video-conference with others, publish materials, see objects at greater magnification than the eye can achieve and remember to take readings during playtime, it will not and cannot replace thinking. As long as computers are not perceived as the way science should be delivered, thus saving on laboratories, equipment and mess, they can add to learning opportunities. Some revision-based sites work because of the repetition and the opportunity to transfer learning into a different setting. The key questions that should be addressed before information technology is used are, 'Does it do something that cannot be achieved without its use?' and, 'Does it do it better than what we already have?' (Not cleaner, or easier but more effectively.) If the activity undertaken in the classroom involves the children in thinking, talking, arguing, measuring, laughing, smelling, hearing, seeing and experiencing in a way that only first-hand experiences can offer, can a program do this and more? Things that are alike are more easily forgotten: endless activities in the same format may not make the links that the brain keeps! Computer science can help learning, but it is not learning in itself.

Summary

Content is important but how it is presented impacts on memory, motivation and thus on learning. Memories can be developed and games can motivate and strengthen memory. When sequencing instructions it is vital to stress key points and organise the information provided, so there is no information overload. Structuring the learning, both in terms of type and delivery, helps retention and retrieval. It is important to use a range of strategies to make learners more receptive, and to remind them of (and revisit) key concepts and vocabulary. Altering lesson length and structure helps learning, alongside organising teaching materials into patterns by using diagrams and charts. Investigations support the learning process because they provide opportunities to return to concepts and ideas. A learning environment that focuses on the task and not on learner ability will support the learning of all groups.

In the next chapter, 'Detective science', the focus is on how investigative approaches can help both learning and learners become more effective.

Putting this into practice

- Keep interruptions to learning to a minimum whilst learners are actively thinking in the independent elements of the lesson.
- Make registration as effective as possible by changing the way materials are introduced.
- Do not introduce too many elements in a lesson as only seven will be remembered (Miller, 1956).
- Make links to everyday life wherever possible to enable the brain to make use of prior knowledge.
- Using games, songs and poems helps with retention and retrieval but ensure the science content is worthwhile.
- Plan learning that will not always be completed in one sitting.
- Decide which key facts need to be told and keep the role of telling to supporting the learning process, not as the learning process itself.

3

Detective science

Learners need to develop an understanding of scientific processes and acquire practical skills to help them make meaning of their learning. In this chapter activities will be provided and where possible these will be illustrated by children's work or photographs to show how promoting detection skills will ensure that learners use their brains to develop their understanding and enjoyment of science. These activities are linked to the theories developed in Chapters 1 and 2, however the focus in this chapter is on the learning and acquiring of skills within classroom settings. The activities are all set in meaningful contexts designed to increase learner motivation. All the examples have been used in classrooms during the past two years. There is a focus on some of those areas of science where different activities can usefully be introduced (as a result of brain-based evidence showing why some current activities do not work). What is suggested here is a rather different approach to learning science, that of the child as detective.

When planning the type of science that children will encounter, the teaching activities and ideas developed should take into account the age and ability of the children. Some published science schemes include activities and ideas that are not matched to how children of a specific age learn. Teachers, as a result, often identify these activities as those that show science does not work. Many feel a duty to follow the activities and plans because they believe they are written by people who have a better understanding of science than they do. When the activities do not result in the planned learning teachers believe it is they who have 'got it wrong'. In reality these activities work in laboratories for trained scientists, but are not pitched at a level which is suitable for most primary school children and there-fore cannot easily be replicated in a classroom situation. The common problem areas are identified here but the approach can be extended to any aspect of science.

Plant growth

In order to understand that plants grow learners need to see changes over time, but they may need help with some of the sequencing issues or being able to identify change and therefore ICT will be useful here (see 'ICT links' at the end of chapter, pp. 55–7). The 'plant in the cup-board' activity is perhaps one of the least brain effective activities that occur in many classrooms across the world. The idea is to prove that plants need light and to do this plants are placed in different places. Sometimes the misunderstanding between a plant's requirement for growth and germination is also included so that learners are given the opportunity to see what happens when the variable light is changed for seeds as well as growing plants.

Plants are generally placed in dark cupboards and on brightly lit windowsills. The problem is that most cupboards are opened at some time and are therefore not continuously dark and the windowsill, even when the plant is not accidentally knocked off, is the hottest place during the day and the coldest place during the night. This tem-perature change can be as great as 20 degrees and this will stress any plant. Stressed plants do not grow any more effectively than stressed learners learn. The stress variable is never considered as it is a discreet variable, but it makes all the difference. If the plants are being given the same amount of water, the plant in the cupboard is exposed to yet more light each time it is watered. What generally happens is the plant in the cupboard does not grow (noticeably) less well and in fact some-times it will look better than the one on the windowsill. As a result, either the plants get switched or teachers will say 'Well, what do you expect – it is science?' Recently in a child's science book the following was written: '*The one in the cupboard should have gon white it did not the one on the windowsill was meant to be best but it lookd dead.*' (Rosie, Year 1)

Growing plants take time for anything noticeable to happen, so there is very little to interest young learners whose brains make small gestalts and they have little prior knowledge in this area. The mem-ory of a small child is short and, unless pictures are taken to support their memory of what the plant looked like before, changes will not be apparent to them. Some of the children will have been absent when the plants were initially set up and this creates further problems. The teacher has a memory that has been developing longer and works over extended periods of time; it is they who set up the activity and therefore will have a greater arousal input. All of this will result in the teacher being better able to observe the changes and it could induce an expectation that the learners will be 'seeing what they see'.

However, in reality things are likely to be different. Chapter 1 indicated that a child's brain is different in size, networks and size of gestalts formed, compared to the brain of an adult, so hiding a plant in a cupboard just ensures that for the average young learner it is out of sight and out of mind. In addition, as no scientific process skills are used when the plants are compared in a general way the registration opportunities are limited. Furthermore, because the learners have little ownership in this activity the end result has little real interest to them. When using 'brain speak', this activity creates only a small level of arousal, small gestalts will be developed and it is unlikely for links to be made to other areas of knowledge. The level of arousal is high for the teacher but low for the learner and this demonstrates an example where teaching and learning do not match.

The brain-based approach

In order to enable learners' brains to be actively involved, it is better to provide plants that have previously been kept in different conditions. In about two weeks most plants will produce effects worth noticing, and then the learners can be asked to use their detective skills to work out what they think has happened to the plants. Support, depending on the age of the learners, can be provided. For instance, young learners can be told that, 'some of these plants have had no water', 'some have had no light' and 'some have had no water and no light but some have been given all they need'. If the children are very young, cards with statements and pictures can be provided for them to attach to the plants when they have made their deductions (see Figure 3.1).

Learners can be provided with measuring and recording equipment and then left to work in mixed ability groups of two or three children. Their task is to decide what they think the conditions were for each plant and to give reasons for their decisions. This approach encourages talking, making judgements supported by reasoning and taking measurements for a purpose. All of these activities will cause links in the brain; children will have ownership of their learning and this will help them to build a picture of what might have happened to the plants and therefore they will begin to understand what plants might need in the future. Primroses are easy to use as they are cheap, difficult to kill and will respond to changes in light and water quickly.

Figure 3.1 Examples of cards for plants

CASE STUDY

In one school Year 4 children were given some primroses that had also been kept under snow. They spent most of a two hour science lesson actively involved in making judgements, detecting what conditions each plant had been subjected to and then justifying their viewpoints to the other groups. Samples of their work are provided in Figures 3.2–3.5. Finally they were challenged to 'rescue' the plants by deciding what they should do to look after them, before planting them in their school garden. On each subsequent visit made to the school the children wanted to talk about how the plants had grown and to point out their progress. The plants were placed in a prominent place in the school garden so that every time the children went to play they walked past the primroses and were reminded of their work. The most effective way of ensuring learning is not forgotten is to provide continuing stimuli.

Continues opposite

Figure 3.2 Children working with plants from different conditions, detecting using their observational skills

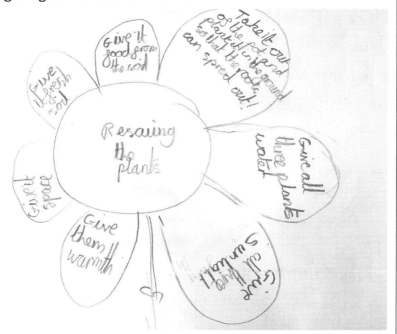

Figure 3.3 Page from a book showing measurements and ideas about plant conditions

Continues overleaf

Figure 3.4 Less literate child's response to the task clearly showing measurements and drawings

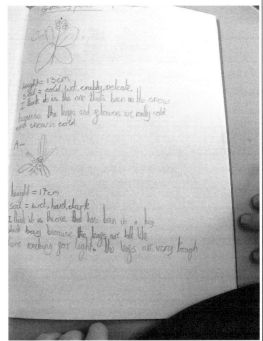

Figure 3.5 Book showing measurements and the child's deductions

Continues opposite

Providing learning in such a way as this will help to make links in the children's brains which are almost like hardwiring as the stimuli are constantly reused. The process of acquiring knowledge is more than the analogy of simply soaking water up with a sponge and hoping when it is squeezed, at a later time, the liquid (information) will flow out: this is similar to activities that just involve learners in watching changes occur over time. It is also important to provide learners with opportunities to solve problems and to talk about their decisions as learning, particularly in the primary phase, is about comparing and combining information for learners whose brains are still developing. The closer in time that the combining can occur then the more likelihood there is of it being successful. This approach requires planning and preparation on behalf of the teacher but the learning stimuli can then all occur in one place at one time, with the comparisons and links being made in a number of linked lessons. Future links will be made when investigative work is also developed from this starting point, for example, by asking learners 'What other things might have made a difference?' and 'How can you find out if your ideas are correct?' If a teacher decides that learners are unsure of what conditions plants might need, they can provide support and help them to plan which variables could be changed in order to see if their ideas are correct.

Detecting germination

Giving learners the role of a science detective is a useful strategy to aid understanding about germination. Placing bean seeds in measuring cylinders is an easy way for the children to see the changes that occur when the beans germinate.

Figure 3.6 A bean seedling

Interestingly, some Year 6 children who were given previously pre-pared bean tubes to look at and to discuss their observations spotted the dates and were puzzled as to why the dates did not, in their view, link to the height of the plant. The tallest one had a 'smaller' date (6/11/05) while the non-germinated bean had a 'larger' date (21/11/05). From a brain-based approach this puzzling and sorting out will cause links to be made with previous learning in science and sometimes other subject areas, as well as experiences and learning from outside school. It also enables the various ideas that learners hold to be discussed and challenged. (The children did not see this problem-solving activity as work!)

When observing and talking to a range of learners about science it is interesting how many times the learners show they are not making links from one area of learning to another. For example, in the seed germi-nation activity it would have been expected that able Year 6 children would immediately see the links between maths (dates) and the growth of plants (science). However they took some time to figure it out, which suggests that perhaps most learning activities often only involve a sim-ple level of learning (small epicentres and small gestalts) rather than promote deep thinking (prior knowledge and aiding hardwiring). The children were also surprised at the way the roots grew and could see lat-eral as well as tap roots; the boys drew very detailed diagrams which they labelled. They identified that the roots came first and then the leaves appeared in pairs. Beyond germination, the children used their observation skills to make decisions about how many days it would take before the bean plant would flower. This approach allows children to use observational drawing and measuring skills, as well as sequenc-ing to look at how seeds germinate, while all the time being involved in discussions. This activity can link into investigative work, with the global question of whether the size of the seed will affect the time it takes that seed to germinate, being asked.

As a follow-up activity it is also possible to see if different types of bean will germinate and grow at different rates, or to have cylinders placed in areas where a range of different temperatures operate. For young children putting the beans in plastic bags on wet cotton wool works really well. These plastic sandwich bags can be pinned on to a display board. Children can look at all the changes simultaneously and so compare and talk about what a bean on Day 10 looks like, as opposed to a bean planted on Day 1.

The success of this approach is that it enables learners to see the big picture and to be able to talk about what they see while making links

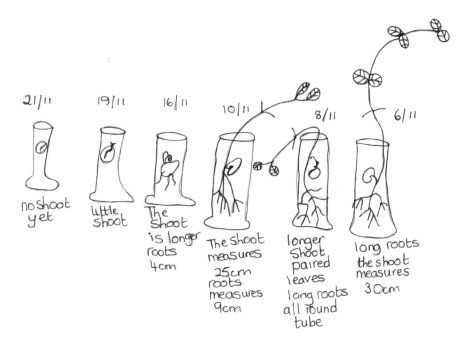

21/11 — no shoot yet

19/11 — little shoot

16/11 — The shoot is longer roots 4cm

10/11 — The shoot measures 25cm roots measures 9cm

8/11 — longer shoot paired leaves long roots all round tube

6/11 — long roots the shoot measures 30cm

Figure 3.7 An example of one child's drawings of beans showing detailed measurements and dates

with previous and out-of-school learning. The approach to solving problems by looking at beans in bags or beans in cylinders seems to reduce the pressure on learners, as there is no single answer and their curiosity is engaged. Seeing the beans or plants often triggers experiences from home or outside school – further establishing brain links and pathways. It is enjoyable to hear some children talk about what they have planted with their grandparents and what they know. This information is not often volunteered in a typical investigative situation where one factor is altered and the idea is to see what changes will occur. Learners will not always relate such work to real life, but may see it as an experiment; '*I do not like it as mine never works and I always get it wrong*' (James, Year 5, Kent LA).

This can result in a rejection of learning in science, as well as reducing opportunities for the retention and retrieval of learning. Unfortunately these feelings are all too common and have been reported elsewhere (see Pollard and Trigg, 2000; Ward et al., 2005).

Although life processes and living things are a very productive area for detective work, these are not the only areas where this approach can be used. The reason why they work so well in this aspect of science is that the natural variability of living things requires a large number of plants to be used to even out the genetic elements and variations. Plants like children are naturally variable. In a classroom situation it is not always possible to grow enough plants to ensure that the results are due to the variables which the children changed rather than the plants themselves. In addition, because the plants are living things they will take time to change and this time makes the learning less successful for younger learners. Some learners will also lose interest in caring for their investigation, as was seen with a group of boys undertaking an investigation on seed germination. They changed the type of seeds but then forgot to water their plants during the week, as '*They are girl things and we wanted to play football*' (Year 6 boys, East Sussex, 2001). Boys do not always dislike plants and one child called Jamie ensured his plant grew well, even though it was the one that was meant not to have water. He carefully explained this in a way that suggested the adult was the one with issues! '*If I had not watered it, it would have died. It was my plant and I want to take it home*' (Jamie, Year 2, Brighton and Hove, 1999).

Cakes and materials changing

Sometimes, because of health and safety reasons, the exciting aspects of science happen away from learners. Baking cakes is a key example of change that means one thing for the teacher and another for learners.

When baking cakes it is likely that a cross-curricular approach will be taken and the activity may be linked to writing lists or instructions in literacy classes. The cake or biscuit making experience excites learners. They are thinking about when it is cooked and what they will do to it, whom they will share it with, or not! The teacher meanwhile is thinking about the science and the changes and probably the mess and sticky fingers! So the learners' gestalts are focused around sharing (or not) and eating, an important feature of young learners' lives. This difference in focus will affect the learning outcome. When young, the days until your next birthday are neverending, while for an adult the year whizzes by – one day it is 1 January and New Year resolutions are being made and then it is the end of the summer term – and the question is where did the time go? Brain research suggests that the difference here is in the way in which the brain works. Where there is the opportunity for large gestalts, time will flow quickly. Where there is little stimulus or the brain is still developing, only small gestalts generally form and, as a result, time will seem to pass slowly.

This does not mean that there is never a time in adult life when time crawls; this may be because there are few stimuli or someone is waiting for an important event to occur and this is focusing their mind so few other thought processes can occur. No wonder the saying is that 'a watched pot will never boil'. This is a good example of time appearing to slow down! By standing by the cooker and monitoring the 'pot', all of one's thoughts are concentrated on that event and hence the brain is focused on a small but temporary gestalt that blocks out other pathways.

When the cake mixing activity is finished and the cakes have gone into the oven to be cooked out of sight, this does not help learners to think about the science of change. The links in the brain are still not made. In order to involve the children's learning capacity provide learners with cakes that have been baked earlier. Make a cake mixture and prepare about ten fairy cakes. Place all but one in the oven in the normal way. After three minutes take one cake from the oven and put it with the uncooked cake. Carry on cooking and remove a cake every three minutes until the last cake is black and hard. Leave the cakes to cool and take photographs. If these can be made into sticky labels all the learners can use them with ease.

ICT

Figure 3.8 Photographs of cakes cooked for different amounts of time

Using these previously cooked cakes, encourage learners to put them into a sequence from the most cooked to the least cooked. By changing the number of cakes and the time difference between taking them from the oven, support for different ages and abilities can be achieved. For example, able or older learners can be given five cakes with slight changes to promote close observation and to challenge their thinking, while for less able or younger learners only three cakes with very obvious differences could be given. The children should decide if they can find out which cake has been cooked for the shortest time. Ask all the learners to talk about the changes they can see. They could also be challenged to answer such questions as, 'How do they know which have been cooked for the longest time?' 'What evidence is there?' As the cakes will never be eaten, let the learners feel and smell them. After talking, comparing and sequencing the cakes, encourage the children to record their findings. (In Chapter 7 advantages and methods of recording to promote learning will be developed.)

This approach will focus the stimuli input by utilising the learners' sight, smell and touch, and registration will change from the social aspects of eating the cake to the science changes involved in the cooking process. By using this method, the changes that occur in the oven are evident and so learners can see what happens when some things are heated. This will help them to make further links between the science and real life. It is suggested that these input stimuli of sight, sound, touch, taste and smell are hardwired so when sight or smells are introduced the brain gets working (a ploy used when supermarkets pump the smell of freshly baked bread into stores). This is not learning, it is an evolutionary response (Fodor, 1983). These senses provide the brain with the same information that helped prevent our caveman ancestors from being eaten by predators. They did not need to think about what to do, they just knew to run! It is important to add learning to this fast-operating and hardwired system. Teachers can do this by providing the learning in clear steps that link together and make each stimuli flow. Making the cakes to eat or take home starts the arousal process, the talking and sequencing of cakes links the stimuli with the cognitive aspect. As the learners compare, sequence and problem solve with these activities, so begins the process of cementing learning. In order to take learning further, at another time other changes that occur when things are heated will need to be discovered, discussed and compared.

After the age of seven many children will start to make generalisations about how heat makes some things change in an irreversible way. For some children the range of stimuli may need to be greater than for others. However, real learning occurs when the links are made and so if cake making is left as a social activity then just as an issue can take over an adult's thinking processes (the boiling pot) so it will be the same for a child (the eating). When the sponge is squeezed later, the science learning will not 'run out', because it was never 'soaked up' in the first place!

Being a detective should be fun, as it enables learners to use their thinking skills and to be able to decide if they understand what they are learning. In order for this to be effective, the activities must have clear learning intentions that are focused at the level of the individual learner. Small learners are not aware of balanced diets and tend to identify things as 'bad', (say, chocolate) or 'good' (for example, an apple). This will not help them to make life choices and is in any case scientifically inaccurate. Although making a plate of food from poly-styrene pieces can be a fun activity, it only allows a child to use what they know or are told. There is often little opportunity to think about what makes a balanced meal.

For example, as a science activity provide the children with pre-prepared lunchboxes or use a picture set (see www.tts-group.co.uk). The information needed is:

1   Humans need food to help them move and keep warm (Red).
2   They need food to grow and to repair their bodies (Orange).
3   They need some food to make their hair shine, nails grow and keep their bodies working effectively (Green).

1   Food for movement and heat includes cakes, sweets and high fat foods (Red group).
2   Food for growth and repair includes meat, dairy produce, fish, pulses, cereals and so on (Orange group).
3   Maintenance needs fruit, vegetables and fibre (Green group).

A simple colour coding of food groups helps to make this clear and allows children to classify and group foods from a young age. In most of the science curriculum, learners do not need to know scientific food groups (such as complex carbohydrates, proteins and vitamins) until after the age of eleven. It is not helpful to eat too much of any one group and a balanced diet contains lots of green, less orange and a little red.

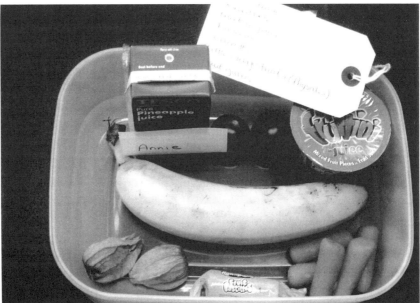

Figure 3.9 Pre-prepared lunchboxes
Structure is needed and do remember not to overload the brain. Reception is needed prior to being a food detective.

Once the basic information has been introduced, learners should then be provided with a pre-prepared lunchbox to investigate and then decide if this person has a balanced diet. The learners can do this by using coloured dots to classify the foods. There will be some foods that cause discussion but this will aid to the learning. Questions might be posed such as, 'Why might a ham sandwich be given an orange code, but a chocolate spread sandwich a red code?' Making up the lunchboxes with more or less ingredients is up to the teacher who will know the learners' level of understanding in the class. Older or more sophisticated learners can compare two lunchboxes and become health detectives, by finding out which is the healthiest lunchbox and why. It is the discussion, talk and debate that will ensure learning occurs and sticks. Additional work could include judging the healthiest lunchbox and giving reasons why it is so from a group of seven lunchboxes. The challenge increases as more information is provided. The ages of the learners should dictate the amount of information provided. Remember, young learners can make links between fewer objects whilst older learners have the ability to make more links.

Looking at a weekly menu could then lead to debate and decisions about eating a healthy diet over time. Using a school menu, each learner can become a 'health detective' and can investigate whether ICT the government's healthy meals proposal is working. They could report their finding in a written newspaper article or orally as a radio or television news feature. Again, the process requires a learner to start by classifying and grouping; for some children real objects will be needed and for others pictures will be fine. Some more challenging issues can be raised using menus for different people.

Breakfast	Lunch	Tea	Supper	Snack
Cereal Skimmed milk Fresh fruit	McDonalds chicken nuggets value meal and an ice cream Diet coke	Fish cooked in white wine sauce, broccoli, carrots and peas. 2 glasses of white wine	Hot milky drink and chocolate biscuit	
Eggs Bacon Sausage Mushrooms	Chicken salad sandwich Apple Orange juice	Baked potatoes with baked beans. Baked apple filled with figs and nuts water	Prune juice	Dried apricots and a small packet of cashew nuts
	Spaghetti bolognaise Garlic bread Glass of red wine		Steak and chips with salad Chocolate pudding and cream	Kit-Kat, bag of crisps and an apple

What one thing would you change for each meal to make it healthier?

Figure 3.10 Which person has the most balanced meal today?

The issue of diet is a complex one and if learners are to make the right choices scientifically as adults do, they will need to be able to discuss and debate from a position of strength and understanding. There are no 'good' or 'bad' foods and even a 'superfood' such blueberries will not make a balanced diet if they are not eaten with other things.

Detecting pre-historic man

There is a suggestion that modern man would never have evolved from primitive man if a change in diet had not occurred. The earliest primates ate a purely vegetarian diet; this required a large gut and the need to eat an intensive amount of vegetable matter. When meat was included into the diet the gut size was able to reduce and so brain size could be expanded. This was important, as the brain requires 22 times more energy than the same amount of ordinary muscle! The size of the brain is dependant on the size of the animal, as bigger animals need bigger brains to coordinate muscles and movement. Humans, however, have bigger brains than many larger animals because the human brain does a lot of thinking and humans are also able to talk. This big brain requires a high-energy diet to ensure it keeps operating. This could only have evolved when a balanced diet including meat was introduced.

Evolution has continued and with the advent of food processing, transport and storage, meat is now no longer a necessity but a choice. Archaeologists and psychologists have used scientific processes and have measured the size of pre-historic skulls to find out what happened in the past. The image of pre-historic man hunting, although prevalent in films, probably did not happen and initially humans were most likely scavengers and ate leftover meat from kills by other animals. Using evidence from bones and skulls to plot evolution is detecting science in its truest sense.

Being a bacteria detective

In the classroom simple but similar detective work can be attempted. Using ideas from the past also provides a good place to start investigating the role of micro organisms. Micro organisms will make things mould; the rate of mould growth and things that prevent mould growth can be detected. Provide learners with sealed Petri dishes containing bread and different solutions. Clear plastic Petri dishes can be used as they are transparent, cheap and can be sealed with super glue or clear adhesive tape. As long as the dishes are thrown away without being opened at the end and no additional bugs are introduced (no touching bread with dirty hands, for example), this is a safe activity to carry out.

It is often sufficient to use dry or damp bread, and then bread with salt, sugar, vinegar, bleach, lemon and honey applied individually. It is also possible to experiment with other things that could be put on bread. Children are told they must be mould detectives and to decide 'Which bread is the mouldiest?', 'Do they all have only one type of mould?', and to make decisions about how they will record and communicate their evidence.

The learners are then left to look at the examples and to make judgements. They will start to find that some dishes have little mould and will ask such questions as, 'Were they all started at the same time?', 'Were they all the same bread?', 'Might they have been put in different places?' All these factors will have been kept the same. When this has been established learners can begin to discuss whether there is something in the dishes that stops mould or makes it grow more.

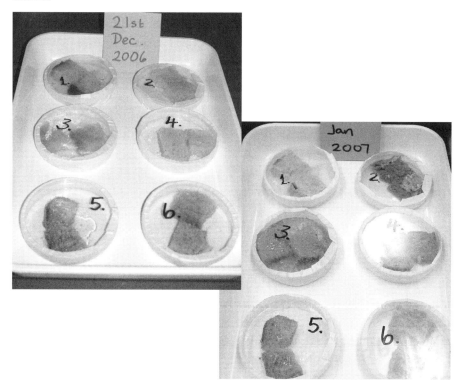

Figure 3.11 Petri dishes

Salt has some effect at slowing mould growth and the concentration is important, but the most surprising liquid to use is honey. Sugar encourages more growth than any other substance and it had been thought previously that honey with its supply of sugar would also have encouraged moulding. However, research by Cooper et al. (2002) showed that honey was three times more effective than an artificial honey solution of the same strength and sugar content. Used in ancient India and other Oriental traditions to heal wounds and with the increase in super bugs, especially those that are resistant to antibiotics, it is possible that honey will make a resurgence as a new super cure.

What time is it Mr Wolf?

How can you tell the time without a watch? Can you use shadows to work out what time it is? Can pictures of shadow clocks be put in the right order? Where is the sun in relation to a shadow picture? Or (a personal favourite) match the shadow to the object. All of these activities require learners to observe, detect and discuss.

Most schools undertake the 'shadow clock' activity; an object or person is put in the playground and chalk is used to outline the shadow. Despite this, many learners still have issues in understanding shadows (the 'sponge' has 'soaked' it up, but the 'water' does not seem to come out when it is squeezed!). Is this because the activity is subject to good weather and requires a day to be spent in the playground with measuring sticks? With other pressures on time this shadow clock activity is unlikely to be undertaken as often as it is needed; three times during the day is thought to be enough to make the point as far as the teacher, with the mature large gestalt brain, is concerned. The shadow moves, they can see it move, game over! It might be that the length of the school day, although this can seem interminable for learners, is too short for a meaningful shadow activity. In order to have any chance of success and to make an impact on learners, the first shadow should be drawn (or photographed) before many children are out of bed (in summertime). The last shadow needs to be measured well after children leave school at the end of the day. Unless this is done the differences are not great enough to make an impact on learners. The arousal is too small to make links that will stay, so no real learning will occur.

ICT Take pictures of a stick in a bottle filled with sand from 7am till 7pm on a sunny summer day. This will require some planning but once undertaken can be used for many subsequent years. The photographs need to be taken every hour throughout the day from the same spot and a measuring or surveyors' tape needs to be included in the pictures. As long as the position remains the same the person taking the pictures can change! These photographs should not have a time on them but should be randomly lettered A to L. They are then given to the children, who need to decide in which order they should go and how they will test their order to see if it is correct. The children need to know that the pictures were taken on the hour and when the first and last picture were taken.

The same equipment used should be available to all learners and the spot from which photos were taken will need to be identified. Learners need to detect what happens and why, compiling evidence to prove that their pictures are in the right order. This is best achieved by the children making relevant measurements themselves. The advantage of this approach is that they can then be asked to measure again at different times of the year and to observe what happens to the shadow, both in size and position.

The mind has evolved in response to selective pressures faced by humans during their evolutionary history, but it is worrying if today's learners are not expected to use their brains to solve problems as they learn but instead are expected to merely 'soak up' facts found out by others. Being a shadow detective involves learners in comparing and combining information, as well as discussing and reasoning their ideas, decisions and opinions – all prerequisites of learning.

ICT ICT links

Using a range of computer equipment can support learners in their detective activities. In the table on page 56 are some uses of ICT to help learners be better detectives.

Activity	Learning
Select six different types of sugar (caster, granulated, brown sugar, Demerara sugar and so on). Dissolve the different types of sugar in water. Evaporate the water off leaving the crystals behind. Use the digital microscope to match the sugar crystals with a sample of the various sugars.	Which sugar was used to make the solutions? Can you use the digital microscopes to solve the problem? Compare, discuss and challenge to find out which sugar was which. As a by-product the children will be introduced again to the fact that dissolving sugar is a reversible change. Let them also look at the sugar solution under the microscope to show it is not possible to see the crystals of sugar when they are dissolved.
Use the digital data logging sensors to take readings of sound, light and temperature over a 24-hour period. This is best if it can be undertaken at three different times during the year. Ask the children to identify what is happening to the readings, what they show and why. To make it simple start them all at the same time of day (this is better when undertaken in a classroom in normal use).	This requires the children to use their decoding skills to work out what is happening. Sounds normally start before dawn breaks as birds will start to sing before sunrise; there will then be light and the temperature will rise. Sound levels might vary throughout the day. Both light and temperature will drop at dusk. Children can see what changes occur at different times of the year. They can use the equipment themselves to test different places and different times. The learning is again achieved by seeing the big picture, something that their ancestors would have been more involved in as they would have had first-hand experience of this. The lifestyles of pupils today ensure they have a sanitised link to their environment.
Match the plant part to the plant. Use a digital camera and enlarge pictures of leaves, stamens and stigma, etc. Use different types of plants and take pictures of seeds also.	Match the pictures to the plants, using flowers, stems and fruit. The children will need to be able to make links and justify their choices. This will again help to provide learning but in a different format and will promote deep thinking.
Use the time-lapse feature on a micro-scope to take a series of pictures of apples or bread drying out, things moulding, or seeds germinating. Ensure that the timeframes of each thing are different (pictures taken at different time lapses).	Ask the children to decide which event happened quickest and which event has the most stages. Label and draw the sequence of events and add scientific words. This again shows the bigger picture of learning in a different format.

ICT

Continued opposite

Activity	Learning
Take a picture of a simple object close up and load it into a PowerPoint program, then copy the picture as many times as you like. Use the shape selector to colour the slide with shapes, which are made blank by using the fill-in selection. For each picture reveal a little more of the object. Play the set of slides as a guessing game.	The children are shown a tiny section of the picture and are asked to guess what the picture might be of. They must then justify their decisions and provide reasons and explanations for the choices they made. This helps to develop language and thinking skills.
Use a picture of an object (black and white is harder) and cut it up to make a jigsaw puzzle.	Ask the children to make up the puzzle without any clue as to what it is. They will need to use their powers of thought, observation and prior knowledge to complete the task. Make the picture link to the area of science being studied, namely a force meter or mass carriers if friction is being studied.
Using an interactive whiteboard, provide the children with a crossword puzzle that links to the area of science being studied.	This helps the children to think about the vocabulary of science and to talk and think together. Make the clues as hard or as difficult as you like. 'Down' words can be easier than 'across' for differentiation.
Take digital camera pictures at high magnification, then take pictures of everyday objects at unusual magnifications. Sand paper at a magnification of $\times 60$ can look like frog spawn.	Using yes and no questions the children have to guess what each object is. They can only ask classification-type questions, such as, 'Is it living?' This will help with their ability to ask relevant questions, will promote links in the brain to what they have seen like this before, as well as develop appropriate vocabulary.
Use a digital microscope picture of a familiar object at high magnification, for example a scarf or woolly jumper. Suggest to the children that the picture is of a strange new land. What animal or plant would inhabit this new world? What would it eat? How would it reproduce? What would its prey be and so on? Depending on the age of the children vary the depth of the activity.	This enables children to use their imagination and to develop an understanding of what plants and animals may need. They will be able to think about life processes and if needs be can research aspects of environments that they may not have remembered. There is no 'right' or 'wrong' way in this activity, therefore the brain will not worry about the outcome. As it develops from a simple starting point all the children will be able to be creative.

ICT

Other detective activities can be developed. All that is required is to ensure that learners are encouraged and are expected to compare, think and undertake the learning processes for themselves (but also by using their group for support). A simple but effective detective activity can be undertaken by focusing on 'graffiti' on a wall. There are five 'suspects', all of whom have in their possession a different type of black marker pen. The children have to use simple chromatography to work out which pen wrote the offending words.

Summary

Learners need to be in control of their learning and the adult's role is to provide the resources and the challenges. These should be as real as possible and motivating as well as fun. Some activities are not brain-based because they do not enable children to make links. All activities should provide a range of opportunities to focus on different stimuli (senses), so that learners are not just reacting to what they see but are also active in making links between all their senses and their prior knowledge. ICT can be used to promote activities, which can then be used by the children themselves. The brain must be challenged, as it runs a powerful and all-purpose program called 'learning'.

Putting this into practice
- Provide scenarios that require learners to discuss, plan, think and challenge their own ideas.
- Ensure there are many options, for example the murderer who left white powder behind – is it the baker, the chemist or the wine maker who did it? Authentic learning is more likely to be remembered.
- Use a skill-based approach so combining and comparisons have to occur, this will result in more neuronal activity and more links being formed.
- Younger learners do not remember many events in the past, so provide learning without the waiting. Things in cupboards or ovens that are out of sight are also out of mind!
- Emotional issues, for example who to eat the cake with, keeping my plant alive, and so on, can influence the learning process. What makes sense to an adult might be interpreted in a different way by learners.

4

Moving and learning

Introduction

In this chapter the use of drama and role-play will be discussed alongside practical classroom-based work. The majority of the chapter focuses on examples of drama and role-play. As these activities develop abstract ideas, the scientific background knowledge has been presented also and because of this the format of this chapter is very different from the rest of the book. The brain likes to have variation so this should be a positive outcome for the reader! It is also designed to enable the activities to be used more effectively in teaching and learning situations.

Although investigative and illustrative activities are a vital part of science, learners also need to understand about models and abstract ideas. Often, due to the very abstract nature of science, these ideas are not delivered effectively through 'chalk or talk' or even practical experiments alone. Drama and role-play, however, provide an effective medium for the development of abstract ideas. Drama also enables learners to be creative and to use their bodies as well as their minds to learn about the world around them.

Role-play is a physical form of modelling and the activities suggested are teacher-directed, but do use modelling as a method of helping learners to visualise and understand abstract concepts, such as dissolving, melting and how sound travels. All the activities here can be used as starting points and there are some suggested extension activities that will enable learners to develop understanding further. Role-play and drama enable learners to work together, sharing ideas and developing their understanding. These activities also provide an

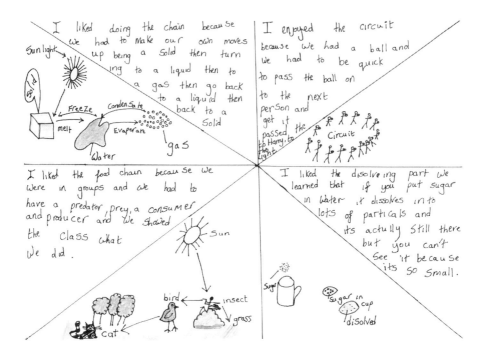

Figure 4.1 James's overview of the drama and his responses to activities taught in this way

opportunity for science learning in a different medium from that of the normal methods. This is important and much needed at a time when many lessons are structured within a predictable three-part format. Learning is less likely to be remembered because of the similarity of this format.

Pica (2004) suggests that most of the brain is activated during physical activity, much more so than when doing seatwork. Drama and role-play involve learners in movement, which is known to develop the links and pathways within the brain (see Chapter 1). Research undertaken on rats showed that movement and exercise made the rats' brains grow, whilst the brains of 'sedentary rats' stayed the same size (see Greenough and Bailey, 1988). However, it is not just the movement element of the work that is important. When using a drama and role-play approach, learners collaborate, talk and debate and all this provides opportunities for learning styles to be developed. This is particularly true if after the event learners are given time to relate what they have learned and experienced to each other through discussions, drawings and written work.

Some ideas to bear in mind

The ideas presented here were undertaken in a number of schools over a period of years, where the focus was on the effective use of drama and role-play in science. The evidence comes from the learners and their teachers and in many cases there was also an improvement in National Test results. This was a by-product and to suggest it was entirely due to the involvement of drama and role-play would be misleading. These strategies were introduced alongside other effective teaching and learning techniques. The focus on science and presenting the learning through a variety of strategies does, however, enable the brain to create many epicentres and strengthen the pathways that make recall easier. The ideas presented here are not intended as hard and fast rules, but rather as things teachers might wish to consider – because over time they have been found to be effective.

Drama and role-play used with other methods

Learners make links with abstract ideas more effectively when they are experienced through a mix of drama, movement and more traditional practical work. The optimum outcomes were experienced when ideas were introduced initially through illustrative, practical work with the drama being used to reinforce the ideas. Finally, the learners were given opportunities to explore the concepts again through engaging in a complete investigation. Many children were able to make the links between the various activities. Indeed, most learners showed a greater sense of understanding when taught through the mixed approach than when either approach was used on its own.

An explanation for this could be that short-term memory relies on an understanding of the information that is received and that this is reinforced when it can draw upon information stored in the long-term memory. This stored information or prior knowledge is vital if true learning is to take place. If a new area of experience is provided to learners then there may be no prior knowledge with which to link the new information. Providing some practical and reception learning first provides prior knowledge; this enables the drama or role 'to make more sense', thus making the learning more likely to stay in the long-term memory.

I think the circulation exercise was the best because we had fun and I really understood it. We were getting really tired but it made me think about how our body works. (Kirsty, Year 5)

Being and seeing

In many cases learners needed to watch what was happening as well as take part. Dividing the class in half or into thirds, depending upon the idea being developed and the space available, was found to be very effective. When learners had a chance to observe others as well as take part, it was found to help reinforce the learning. This might be because learners received a 'double dose', and thus a greater registration, by both doing and seeing. Anecdotal evidence suggested some learners were so involved in their part in the drama or role-play that they were unable to see the bigger picture and this only became apparent when they watched others or reviewed photographic evidence of the session.

ICT

> I like being a gas particle and bouncing round, the pictures of when we was in different states helped as you could really see what we looked like. (Gary, Year 5, Kent)

Props, tabards and time to download

Props and costumes help learners 'get into role' as well as providing some additional registration when photographs are taken. Photographs also help with retention and retrieval as they can be used for prompting discussion at a later time as well as providing clarity for what is happening then and there. The props can be made simply out of card, although coloured tabards have proved particularly effective in many of the activities suggested. Talking about the activity afterwards is important but it is useful for the learners to download their experience in other ways, providing them with an opportunity to discuss their activities with each other, for example, whilst drawing or writing a poem. It seemed this helped them make more sense of what they were involved in and enabled learners to remember and discuss the activities at a later time. It also allowed a free choice in whether to produce an annotated drawing, to write an account or to make a rap, which promotes autonomy and the opportunities to be creative.

Whilst recording does not have to be immediate, the closer to the time of the drama the more effective the memory traces will be. One of the interesting things found from working with these learners was their ability to remember what they had learnt often more than six weeks after the activity. The majority of learners were found to be enthusiastic about the activities and were able to talk about what they had liked and what they had learnt. Katie, a Year 5 pupil, initially considered science as the subject she least enjoyed. However, at the

Figure 4.2 Phoebe's evaluation of three drama activities: Phoebe enjoyed the snowman most and although the heart and circulation system was viewed as boring, it was awarded 8/10

end of a drama and science lesson she stated '*I had fun through the whole of the science lesson!*'

To support drama in the classroom the following ideas have been provided. The format is kept the same for ease of use. Key vocabulary has been identified in **bold text**. Some subject knowledge is given to help support teaching but try not to give this to the learners in its entirety as they might be overloaded! Remember the seven, plus or minus two rule (Miller, 1956). Health and safety is not described in detail but teachers need to think about this in regard to their own setting and learners. Generally it is important to think about footwear and how learners can make their actions safe for themselves and their classmates.

Because of the nature and size of this book only a limited number of more challenging aspects of science are exemplified here. They begin with some examples from life processes and living things. This is fol-

lowed by some linked ideas focusing upon materials and their properties and finally some examples from physical processes are introduced.[1]

Food chains and webs

Key learning points here are:

- food chains represent energy transfer in a system
- all chains start with the sun
- 'predator', 'prey', 'consumer' and 'producer' are words that
  describe the food chain.

Practical tasks

Prior to this work learners should have been researching a number of
food chains. They should have identified one animal and found out
both what it eats and what eats it. They should be reminded about the
role of plants. Words like 'primary and secondary consumer', and
'predator' and 'prey' should have been introduced to them.

Vocabulary

Predator, prey, food chain, energy, **consumer, producer**, leaf, secondary consumer, primary producer, primary consumer environment,
habitat, herbivores, carnivores, omnivores, **sun**

Background knowledge

The energy that is utilised by all people to run, walk, keep warm and
carry out their mental functions is derived from the food they eat. Other
animals do not regularly eat humans, but in some environments
humans could provide food for animals such as lions, tigers or polar
bears. The food that is eaten is the source of energy. Humans are
omnivorous, that is that they eat a range of plant and animal material.
Some animals only eat plant matter, they are called herbivores, whilst
other animals will only eat other animals, and they are carnivores. Light
energy from the sun starts the food chain; plants manufacture food
using this light energy. The food factory is in the leaves and the process
requires light, oxygen and water. These ingredients are turned into a
type of sugar, which plants use for growth, respiration and all other life
processes, with any extra being stored.

---

[1] A full set of detailed teaching notes with photographs is available from
www.puttinglearningfirst.com

It is wrong to think that plants breath in carbon dioxide and give out oxygen. Plants use oxygen to break down food, to release energy for all its functions in the same way that all living things do. However, at the same time a process called photosynthesis is carrying out the reverse operation by using carbon dioxide to make sugar. These two separate processes occur during the day, while at night plants can only carry out respiration as there is no sunlight for making food.

A plant is a primary producer as it uses sunlight to generate food. It can be eaten by a primary consumer, an animal that eats plants in order to use its stored energy for its own life processes. The primary consumer could be the prey for a predator; for example, a snail will eat the leaves of garden plants and will become dinner for passing birds. The bird is a secondary consumer and is also a predator. In turn, the bird may become a meal for another larger bird (often called a bird of prey) or it could be eaten by a cat.

In the environment, the links between plants and animals are not linear; snails will eat many types of plants, as most gardeners know, and there are many hundreds of types of birds, not all of which are found in our gardens. Other animals eat snails (one is a killer caterpillar, *Hyposmocoma molluscivora*!).

The way energy is spread through the system is called a food web rather than a simple chain. However, the web is made up of many simple chains. The programme of study here initially requires learners only to understand simple chains. Because less than 10 per cent of the energy is stored in any one link in the chain for the next link to use, it is important to have many more producers than consumers. In secondary school the biomass pyramid will be developed.

Resources

Tabards of different colours (including yellow) and labels for learners to name their own organisms.

Activity description

Depending on the age group, either present the learners with roles from a known food chain or ask them to show their understanding by using a simple food chain of choice. After giving them some time to discuss and practise their roles, ask them to then perform for other groups. Ask the audience such questions as, 'Which is the primary producer?' or 'Which is the predator or the prey?' Learners will use this vocabulary with constant practice and this is best in a situation where they are comfortable.

Next, provide learners with the names of organisms in a food chain and ask them to decide producers and consumers, prey and predators, by using the clues. They can then create food chains with clues; for example, 'I make my food from the sun, and slugs, snails and caterpillars eat me', or 'I cannot make my own food, I am herbivorous and enjoy eating the leaves of many types of plants'.

Extension tasks

Provide learners with named animals and plants from a local environment and help them to make a food web. Questions can be posed such as, 'What would happen in the environment if people use poison to kill the slugs and what would be the result across the habitat?'

Other ideas for life processes

- The heart and circulation system
- The role of bacteria in causing illness and the use of medicines and the human immune system in fighting them
- Growing plants – dance drama of the seed (under sevens)
- The life cycle of plants (over sevens)
- The role of micro organisms in mould and decay

In Figure 4.3, Kirsty has shown the parts of the body but her picture does not include the children who were the blood. The blood took red paper (representing oxygen to the muscles from the heart. The muscles exchanged these for blue paper, the waste products, and the blood returned to the heart and from there to the lungs, where oxygenated blood stared the process again. This can be developed further with older learners.

The snowman – how insulation keeps things cold

- to know that insulators slow down the movement of heat
- air is a gas. Gasses are good insulators

Practical tasks

Melting and freezing water, taking temperature readings, wrapping ice balloons in material and seeing the effect, preserving an Ice troll (frozen water bottle with a face drawn on) – all these are activities that can be used before or after drama.

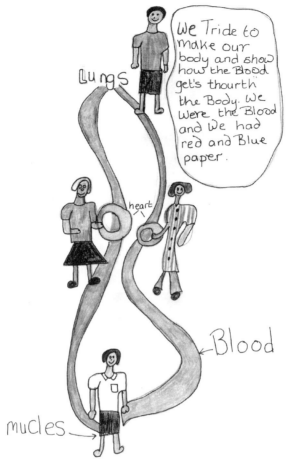

Figure 4.3 Heart and circulation system drawing by Kirsty

Vocabulary

Cold, **hot**, **melting**, **freezing**, capacity, volume, hard, smooth, **solid**, **liquid**, particles, **movement**, heating, cooling, coat, heat energy, **insulation**, conductor, air temperature, thermometer

Background knowledge

Learners usually think that materials are hot or cold. They do not understand about heat energy and use words drawing on everyday use. As a result a very faulty model of insulation is developed. Young children are told to put a coat on when it is cold to keep them warm, so it is not surprising that when asked what will happen to a snowman with a coat on (see concept carton; Keogh and Naylor, 2000) they will suggest the snowman will melt.

Heat energy is not visible and there is no such thing as cold. Cold is the absence of hot! If a coat is placed around a snowman on a winter's day the snowman will be colder than the surrounding air temperature. Heat always travels from areas of high energy (hot) to areas where there is low energy (cold) to equal things up. However, the coat is made of a material that makes it difficult for the heat to pass through (insulator) and so it will keep the snowman cold for longer. Eventually the heat will be conducted and the snowman will melt. Putting a coat on when it is cold does keep a child warm, but the heat is coming from them and the coat is preventing it from being passed into the air as easily.

Resources

One child to be the snowman, red tabards representing hot, coloured tabards to represent the coat.

Activity description

Remind the children about the properties of solids, liquids and gases. They should know that solids have a fixed shape and fixed volume and that the snowman is solid ice. First have the snowman without the coat and allow the heat energy from the sun to melt the snowman. Next surround the snowman with a coat, which prevents the heat energy from getting into the snowman. The heat energy will try to get to the snowman but the coat will insulate it and the heat energy will not easily get through. Ensure that eventually some heat is able to get through; a coat will only slow down melting but not completely prevent it from happening. Ensure learners understand about heat energy making the solid change to a liquid and that the insulator slows down the process.

Extension tasks

Ask the learners to act out different scenarios, including melting ice pops, wrapping frozen peas, or an ice-lolly on a hot day and so on. Ask them to think of other everyday examples where insulation works and to act out how this works. Use this as an assessment opportunity. If the learning is secure, introduce the idea of insulation keeping things warm.

Candles burning – irreversible chemical change

Key learning points here are:

- that some changes are irreversible
- when chemical changes occur new materials are formed
- burning is an irreversible chemical change.

Practical tasks

Provide an opportunity for learners to look at candles placed in sand trays. Make observations of the flame whilst the candle is burning, measure changes in mass. It is also helpful if the learners have carried out supported activities as described in Chapter 2.

Vocabulary

Solid, liquid, gas, wax, melting, burning, irreversible change, chemical change, oxygen, colourless gas, water vapour, carbon dioxide, mass, decreasing

Background knowledge

Candles need a source of oxygen in order to burn. When there is no oxygen there will be no flame. The candle itself is composed of hydrogen and carbon. A candle needs an absorbent wick, which will let the liquid wax move through it and provide a source of flame. When the wick is lit the heat from the match causes the wax to melt, changing from a solid to a liquid, and this liquid is then drawn up the wick and changes into a gas; it is this gas vapour that is burnt.

Learners often think that it is the wick that is being burnt. A lit candle if left alight will eventually burn down. All the wax will have joined with the oxygen in the air to form two invisible gases. One of these is carbon dioxide and the other is water vapour. If the flame is blown out after the candle has been lit for some time, the wick will continue to produce candle vapour. This vapour is white in colour, smells like candles and is often mistaken for smoke. Candles are an example of an irreversible chemical change.

Resources

Tabards of green and yellow to represent the candle and blue or white tabards to represent the oxygen in the air.

Activity description

Start with the nine learners – six wearing green to represent hydrogen and three wearing yellow who are carbon. The nine children who are oxygen are surrounding them. When the wick is lit the candle will start as a solid but will melt quickly, becoming a liquid; here the heat will turn them into a gas and at that point they will burn and form a new substance with oxygen. Many learners know that carbon will form carbon di (meaning two oxygen) oxide; explain that this means the carbon has one oxygen on each hand. Those representing the (green) hydrogen atoms will have to find one oxygen to share between them (hydrogen and two oxygen). When they link with oxygen they will move away from the candle. Eventually there will be no candle left to burn.

Extension tasks

Introduce what will happen if the candle is very drippy; the melting temperature is low and instead of all the wax being turned into a gas the liquid will run away from the source of the heat and will turn back into a solid.

Ask the learners to perform a drama where they show what would happen if the oxygen ran out.

Other dramas for materials and their properties

- Solid, liquid and gas dance
- Why things dissolve
- Why things do not dissolve
- The drama of the filter paper
- The periodic table

The solid, liquid and gas dance is explained in many books and on websites. In Figure 4.4 a child shows their version of how they take part in the dance by drawing the organisation of particles in the different states; using music during this drama helps learners with the movement of particles.

Sounds travelling

Key learning points here are:

- that sounds travel as vibrations
- that sounds travel better through a solid than a liquid and better through a liquid than a gas
- that sounds will not travel in a vacuum.

Figure 4.4 Solid, liquid and gas

Practical tasks

Provide opportunities to make and use string telephones and perform explorations with sounds travelling in different mediums (namely solids and liquids as well as air).

Vocabulary

Sound, vibration, solid, liquid, gas, further, **louder,** quieter, vacuum, space, **particles,** passing, compression, wave

Background knowledge

Many young children believe that sounds travel better through a gas than any other material. This is because they hear in air (a gas) and will say that when trying to talk under the water the bubbles get in the way.

After undertaking the solid, liquid and gas dance it is helpful to use their understanding of the properties of these states of matter to show how the organisation of atoms in materials can help to explain properties like sound travelling. In a solid, the atoms are closely packed and the bonds are strong. In liquids the atoms are less organised, and in gases the atoms (particles) are spread further apart.

Sounds travel as a series of vibrations starting at the source of the sound. So when a drum is hit, the hitting is the energy that makes the drum skin vibrate. This energy is converted into the kinetic (movement) energy of the particles. When the particles are close together the movement of the energy is quick and easy. Sounds will therefore travel better in solids than in liquids, and better in liquids than in gases.

Some hard, rigid materials like metal conduct sounds effectively because the particles are organised in a set way; other solid materials like cork or cotton are poor conductors of sound as whilst they are solid their bonds and organisation ensure that the energy cannot be passed from particle to particle effectively. Sound will travel at the same speed regardless of the loudness of the sound (whether it is loud or soft), but sounds do travel further on hotter days (as particles have more energy).

Sounds travel by movement of the particles and this transfers energy. Eventually the energy will not be sufficient to carry on moving the particles and the sound will diminish. The nearer the particles are together and the more rigid the material, the easier it is for the energy to pass, as less is converted into the kinetic movement of the particles themselves. Also the louder the sound, the more energy it has to begin with, so the further it will travel.

Activity description

Ask the ten particles to line up in the organisation of a solid, all facing towards the front. They should be very close together and it is important to ensure there is nothing behind the last particle that they could fall onto.

Push the shoulder of the first particle very gently, telling them that the object making the noise causes a vibration. The first particle will knock into the particle behind and the sound (push) wave will travel towards the end of the line. Those watching will see it move and those taking part will feel the movement.

Next show what would happen if there were a louder sound. This requires a bigger push on the first particle; the sound should travel further and make the particle move more. Do the same with the organisation of a liquid, then a gas.

The nearer the particles are together the further the sound will be able to travel, and that the harder (louder) the original sources of vibration the further it will travel. Swap over with the next group of ten learners and repeat until all groups have undertaken the task.

When all the particles have had a turn and are sat down ask what would happen in outer space?[2]

---

2 There are no particles so there is no sound. Sound will not travel in a vacuum.

Extension tasks

Some solids are better conductors of sound than others. Using drama show how sounds travel through a range of different materials. Provide props if needed.

Light passing through some materials and shadow formation

Key learning points here are:

- light travels through transparent materials
- light cannot travel through opaque materials and shadows are formed
- some materials will bounce light
- light travels in straight lines.

Practical tasks

Learners should be given opportunities to look at many objects and see which ones let light pass through and which ones do not. They can then draw and measure the sizes and shapes of shadows. They should sort materials into those that are transparent and those that are opaque.

Vocabulary

Transparent, **light**, **opaque**, translucent, bent, **reflection**, bouncing, scattering, **light**, dark, **absence of light**

Background knowledge

Light is a form of energy, it can pass through some materials and be blocked by others. Materials that let light through are said to be transparent, whilst materials that stop light from travelling through them are said to be opaque. Translucent materials let some light through but the light pathway is distorted and some light is scattered back; as a result the light source cannot be clearly seen.

The reason why materials let light travel through them is due to the properties of the materials at a particle level. If the learners have already experienced the solid and gas drama, it is possible to use this information to show how in a solid the particles can be close together but will have gaps between the particles for light to travel through, whilst in other materials the gaps between the particles are not regular and organised so although the light might travel through one layer the next layer of material will stop the movement of the light, blocking its pathway.

Some materials (those that are reflective) bounce all the light back. If the material is so smooth that the light is bounced back as a complete parcel a reflection is seen. If the surface is rough the light is bounced all over the place (scattered) and no image will be seen. If the light is stopped from travelling through a material a shadow is formed.

Resources

Tabards and cardboard arrows to show the way light travels.

Activity description

Start with a simple shape of a solid but where there is a clear pathway between the particles to let the light get through. Place learners in a regular formation with well-defined gaps between the rows and all rows having the same gaps. The five learners playing the role of light will be able to get though the material to the other side.

Reorganise the rows so that the gaps in one line are blocked by a particle in the next line. Ask the light to try and get through; they will get stuck and there will be no light behind, so a shadow will form. Swap the groups over and ask the learners to show a material that will not let light through; use only one learner to represent the light trying to go through the material and make the others go around the outside of the shape. When they are on the other side ask them to stop. Ensure they have not walked behind the shape and are showing that the light goes around the outside but not through, so there is a space behind the object where the light has been blocked which is a shadow.

Split the class into small groups and show them objects that they have experimented with before in class. Ask them to act out what they think would happen with the light for each of these objects.

Extension tasks

With very able learners demonstrate a reflection. The light will come towards the surface and this light will be bounced back in exactly the same way. If a surface is bumpy this bouncing makes the light go in all directions and no image will be seen. Ask the learners to think about a puddle or lake on a still day as compared to a windy day.

Other ideas for dramas on physical processes

- Electrical circuits
- The Earth, Sun and Moon and their orbits
- Magnetism repelling and attracting
- Magnetism – the theory of domains

Figure 4.5 An electrical circuit

In Figure 4.5 Charlotte shows how the electrons, represented by balls, are held by the children in a circuit. They are passed when the circuit is complete. This shows how lightbulbs will light immediately the circuit is closed, as the electrons are already in the wires and are ready to move. It can also be used to show how when insulators are in a circuit the electrons are present but cannot move. If a switch is opened, learners cannot pass the balls. It takes learners some time to get used to passing and receiving balls at the same time.

Other uses of movement

With younger children their bodies can be used to explain their understanding of scientific words, for example stretching, bending, attracting, repelling, pushing, pulling and friction. Drama with young children should focus on the everyday observable features of science, like plants growing, the movement of animals or how different materials might behave. Some learners can show loud sounds by using their bodies and can contrast these with quiet sounds. When moving, learners are making links in their brains; it is a different way of working and is highly motivating. Young learners can act out why some materials are waterproof, why the brick house withstood the wolf, as well as showing how electricity needs a complete circuit by joining hands and playing pass the squeeze. In order for the squeeze to travel in the circuit all the hands must be joined.

Older learners can start to use drama to develop an understanding of abstract ideas. Many of the ideas here are of an abstract nature. The drama helps to reinforce the practical tasks. With older learners role-play can also be used to make and reinforce learning, by debating about how companies pollute water or by taking roles in a scenario based on how changing land use in some areas of the world may impact on indigenous populations. Currently in the news is the issue of global warming or the eradication of species. The use of expert witnesses can provide an audience for research. Reporting scientific investigations as news reports will ensure retention, as the content is usually rehearsed and practised!

CASE STUDY

Assessment

In some lessons it is possible to use drama to understand what misconceptions the learners hold. A group of Year 5 children was asked to role-play a food chain. They had choices about equipment, labels, props and simple costumes. One food chain consisted of the sun, an apple tree, a boy, an eagle and a lion. One child acted out the sun giving energy to make the apple tree grow; in turn this was transferred to the boy when he ate the apple. He was then killed, but not eaten by the eagle. The lion hunted the eagle but never caught it. The children were acting out aspects of animal behaviour within a habitat, but without the real understanding of energy transfer up a food chain. Contrast this with the group who showed a simple chain. Here the sun's energy was used to make the grass grow; this energy was transferred to a snail that ate some grass. The snail was then was eaten by a bird, and finally the energy from the sun found its way to the cat that caught and ate the bird.

Each group was able to devise their own chain and then demonstrate it to the rest of the class. The group observing then had to give feedback; what was good and if there were any issues. This opportunity to discuss with each other and other groups helped move the children's ideas forward. It also helped the teacher identify where problems existed.

Summary

Movement helps learners make links in the brain. It is a different way of teaching science and is motivating for learners. Learners demonstrate a higher level of engagement and enjoyment when undertaking drama; this can prevent a rejection of science learning. Encouraging learners to develop their own drama will provide evidence for assessment.

Putting this into practice
- Allow learners to collaborate, talk and debate as part of the process.
- Ensure the movement element is reinforcing learning already provided, to make the most effective use of prior knowledge and long-term memory.
- Use photographs to enable learners to see the big picture.
- Change the type of experience provided with the age of the learners; abstract concepts and ideas work more effectively with older learners, whilst younger learners can use movement to reinforce observable features.
- Use drama for extending as well as assessing understanding.

5

Word, words, words

In their most recent report on the curriculum the QCA (2006) high-lighted that children's ability to use scientific vocabulary was not improving even though more time had been spent on developing literacy skills. It is thought that this lack of understanding will impact on children's understanding of science at later key stages. Teachers have also identified this lack of progression but are unable to provide a reason. It is well known that words used in everyday life often have a different scientific usage. Current practice is not leading to improvements, so perhaps it is time to do something different! This chapter suggests some alternative approaches.

Language development in babies and young children is both rapid and fascinating; overall the most rapid development is in the first two years. Between birth and three months babies will make 'cooing' sounds and laughing is usually adopted by six months. By nine months babbling with sounds and simple words like 'ma, ma' and 'da, da' are common. Babies also begin to point when using these and the first identifiable words are spoken at around the age of 12 months. For the next six months or so, on average, two words are added per week to the vocabulary. At 18 months children can usually identify and name body parts, animals and have some simple social language such as, 'bye, bye'. By the age of two years, language has developed fast, with 'What's that?' being the order of the day and repetitive stories being much loved. The brain is developing the hardwiring needed to enable the learner to communicate; although producing only small gestalts, the regularity and repetitive nature of early language make links that stay. The average two–three year old has a vocabulary of about 150 to 300 words and can ask 'Why' questions! By four 'can't' and 'wont' have been learned, along with many other new words, to give them a total bank of between 800 and 1000 words. By the time most children start school a bank of 2000 words will be present and used, although deciphering language can sometimes be problematic for teachers. By the end of Key Stage 1 further development will have taken place and eight years-olds in general will know and use around 11,000 words. Growth will not stop here and it is thought that adults generally have a repertoire of more than 50,000 words (Hirsh-Pasek et al., 2006).

Language in school may be very different from language used at home and in most typical classrooms teachers use a range of everyday and science words. Take for example the word furniture; this is not a science-specific word but one used regularly in schools. Some young children have not yet realised that this is the common name for a collection of chairs, tables and the like. Because the language of home may be very different from the language of school, it is possible there is no prior knowledge and thus nothing to draw upon and to attach new learning to. In addition, there is the language of science! So it is not surprising that Lemke (1990: 24) suggested that learning science is like learning a foreign language, and to be fluent in that language requires regular practice in both speaking and listening. In other words, learners need to become immersed in it.

As with the new words of a foreign language, in science learners have to read the word whilst 'reading' the world (Friere, 1991), only becoming confident when they can read the word and also understand its meaning. The word has nothing to be associated with, so there will be little retention or retrieval. Those learners who can decode the word but do not understand are likely to think they cannot do science and will demonstrate elements of non-consideration. Science-specific vocabulary can be confusing for the learner, and as a result they may develop two sets of languages: one for school science and one for the rest of their life.

A good example of this is the term 'force': force in everyday life is where someone makes you do something you do not like, or it sometimes means the army, the navy and the air force. Force in science is even more problematic as the forces themselves are invisible and only their effects can be seen. Most adults have problems defining the term 'force'! In order to have a language of science, that is understood both at school and in the wider world, the learner must assimilate by adding it to what they already know. Without this there will be no true learning as language is the medium through which learners learn (Piereira, 1996).

Able learners use language modelled to them by their teachers or other adults. They learn this from about two years of age. Babies (and some suggest teenagers) only focus on what interests them! Current research has suggested that it is only at the age of two that children realise it is what a speaker says that should be focused on, rather than on what interests them. In some cases although the language or word is heard its meaning might not be interpreted. Children can and do use words they hear, but often without any understanding of the meaning. This can be seen in the classroom when young children use the word 'gravity'. They may have heard it and they may know that it keeps things on the ground, but their understanding of this invisible force is unlike that of the scientific community. Children can perceive gravity, as in '*Like God, it is everywhere, it does not have a set place*' (Year 3 boy) or '*It is in the air, it pushes you down to the ground. That is why on the moon there is no gravity, there is no air and in space people have to wear big boots to keep them from floating away*' (Year 3 girl).

It is far more useful to leave scientific words like gravity that have concepts attached to them until learners have used everyday language to explain what happens. Instead of using 'gravity' straight away, a typical sentence that describes gravitational attraction should be used instead, for example,

> *We are held onto the planet by an invisible pull, it is inside the Earth and it holds us on to its surface and pulls things down towards it.*

This is a mouthful but it will help learners to understand the ideas behind the word, rather than just attaching the label. 'Dissolving' therefore becomes

> *When salt is put into water, the salt breaks down into very small pieces and mixes. The size of the pieces means it cannot be seen with the naked eye but we know it is there because we can taste it. This also happens with other substances that are added to water. Can you think of any?*

Most scientific terms, like gravity, condensation, evaporation, eclipse and vibration, are shorthand to describe an abstract concept. Thinking that young learners understand this concept because they can say the word is part of the problem that comes with learners attaining scientific language at an early age.

CASE STUDY

Vibrators

A group of Year 4 children was given opportunities to find out about sound; they were not initially formally taught the word 'vibration' but were enabled to see and feel vibrations happening. They began to talk about when some thing 'wobbled' and how it 'tingled' and that it 'moved or tickled' depending on where they placed the tuning forks. They were not given any formal language at this point in the lesson, as it was the exploration stage of an introductory lesson to the topic.

Before the exploration had finished a group of visiting advisors and governors came into the class and asked the children what they were doing. They told the visitors they were finding out about sound. One of the children was asked by the chairman of the governors, who was the local vicar, what a tuning fork was. The child immediately responded, 'I think it is my vibrator!' It took some time to later explain to the governors that as the children had heard of vibration before but were not sure what it meant, it was to be expected that they would use terms in incorrect ways. It is possible that everyday language and science were also being confused, but this point was not developed further!

This case study also highlights why it is important that all equipment is introduced by its correct name at the start of the lesson, and that learners are enabled to explore potential uses. Such an approach provides learners with opportunities to use language as they work. For learners to really understand specific language they first need to develop an understanding of the concept and then the word can be slotted in later. When learners explore sound and vibrations they often make the link between a 'sound' and a 'wobble' or a 'tickle'. However, sometimes it is hard to see the wobble[1] but its effects can be felt. Learners need to use tuning forks to splash water from saucers, to speak against a blown-up balloon and feel their voice, to watch and make ping pong balls bounce when they are brought near a vibrating object and to observe rice bouncing on a sheet of clingfilm held above the surface of a drum.[2] These examples reinforce the ideas held and if the concept is understood – it wobbles when a sound is produced and if something stops it wobbling, for example when a hand is put on a chime bar, the sound stops – then learners will understand the concept of how sound is produced. The scientific term 'vibration' can then be introduced. This ensures a range of opportunities to make links

---

[1] This is because of the number of vibrations per minute. A middle C tuning fork will vibrate 256 times a second, much too quick for the eye to see, but enough to tickle and tingle an ear lobe!

[2] Learners may find rice bouncing on a drum confusing, but seeing the vibrations travel to clingfilm held above with rice on it really reinforces the idea that the rice moves because of the vibrations.

within the brain; it will help not only with retention, but also with retrieval. Splashing your friend with water using only a tuning fork has been found to have high registration! It also helps if words used during the session are then displayed visually. Pictures with words can be added as a topic develops.

The rush to give scientific words to young learners sometimes seems to be directly equated with thoughts about the improvement of knowledge. Young children do like big words and a range of exciting vocabulary is important but some words are just naming words, like 'diplodocus', 'Tyrannosaurus Rex' and 'Newton metre'. These need to be introduced alongside the object. Other words are more complex as they will describe a process or event and often one that is not tangible. Using practice developed in other areas can sometimes help, for example, when measuring in mathematics, learners are not given standard units to start with but use straws, bricks, blocks, hands and feet until they realise that a common system is useful. In science a common way of communicating is also needed; it is too long-winded to say that 'water gains enough energy to turn into a gas and becomes a vapour', when the shorthand 'evaporation' is available. However, to be fully understood the non-standard experience is required first. Wellington and Ogbourn (2001) suggested that teachers need to put concepts into words that children understand and this requires everyday language to be used initially by both adult and child. This finding is reinforced by many researchers and research projects and is not new. In fact, in 1996 Ogbourn and colleagues suggested that all learners needed to use everyday language and everyday contexts in order to make sense of scientific concepts and experiences.

Four simple rules for language development

In order to help learners with the language of science four basic rules should be considered.

1 That vocabulary should always be taught in context and linked to prior knowledge.

When working within a scientific topic, learners need to be given opportunities to match the objects or equipment with labels, words or pictures. They need to be allowed to fix physical labels to help make a mental link. This does happen in many Early Years settings and classrooms but the theory is the same whatever the age; brains are wired in the same way! The first type of vocabulary that learners need to learn is the common word for everyday things. Later, in the case of complex science vocabulary, they need to see how this links with what has already been taught. The complex science vocabulary, such as the names of unusual animals, plants and environments, should be taught on a need-to-know basis that begins with, 'What do they really need to know to start with?' So knowing that *Quercus robur* is the formal name for the common oak is not required, initially, any more than knowing there is more than one type of oak tree. It is networks that are useful in using the brain for deep learning and the ability to use the knowledge. All language should focus on words that can be taught in context, that have meaning for the learners and are those to which they will be exposed on a regular basis when learning about a particular aspect of science. It is vital to keep things simple before adding more detailed examples.

All learners are different and language acquisition is as important in older learners as in infants. Understanding learners need is vital, so while some children come to school already having a good general understanding of basic vocabulary and might only need specific naming words, such as 'glass', 'metal' and 'wood', others might need to start with everyday terms. In secondary education learners could be struggling with terms such as 'elements', 'atoms' and 'periodicity'. The rules of language development are the same; language needs to be taught in a context that is understood, with simple words first introduced together with picture clues. Vocabulary lists are not found to be productive (Brozo and Simpson, 1998), particularly if they do not link with real examples. Lists of words and their definitions are helpful for teachers as they already have the language and understanding and so they will provide a prompt or cue to memory. Learners do not have the same starting point and have few if any memory traces associated with these lists, and so the list of words and definitions can easily be forgotten.

2 In order to develop vocabulary, active learning techniques are required.

Learners need to make associations for themselves. Even complex things like elements in the periodic table are understood more effectively if learners are actively involved. In one science activity learners are labelled as an element by having a PE hoop around their middle that has the name and number of electrons for that element attached. It is surprising the number of trainee teachers who have been taught about atomic numbers but do not remember or really understand what this means. As a result they have not been able to make the next step in their learning. Enacting the periodic table together with words and symbols helps learners with the vocabulary and how the words are used in context.

A class of Year 2 children was introduced to a simple melting activity using clear plastic bags that contained a small amount of an everyday substance inside. They were able to put the bags (with butter, lard, jelly and chocolate) into hand-hot water in jugs on their table. They watched the changes and recorded which material melted first. They talked about what they saw but were not really using any science words.

On the board a range of word cards had been produced and laminated. These included 'heating', 'cooling', 'melting', 'solid', 'liquid', 'hot', 'cold', 'changing', 'heat'. When the children had seen the materials melt they took them from the water and placed them on the table in the order in which they melted. They left the bags on their table when they went out to play.

When they came back the materials had gone back to their original 'hard' form. The children then sat on the carpet and the word cards were used to help scaffold an account of what they had seen. The teacher told the children she was going to talk to them about the activity and they should use one of the science words in their answer. If they could, they should stand up and hold the word. They were challenged to see if they could use all the science words.

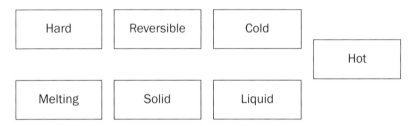

She used the following series of questions and focused only on the melting chocolate to begin with.

T 'Let's talk about what happened and use our words to explain what we saw happen.'
T 'What was the chocolate like at the start?'
C1 'It was solid.'
C1 stood up and put 'solid' at the start of the science word sentence.
T 'What word could you use to describe the water in the jug?'
C2 'It was hot water.'
C2 came out to hold the 'hot' card.
T 'Then what happened?'
C3 'The chocolate melted.'
C3 held 'melted' next.
T 'Was the chocolate still the same as at the start?'

Continues opposite

CASE STUDY CONTINUED

C4 'No it had gone runny.'
T 'Is there a card that we could use?'
C4 'Yes, liquid.'
C4 took 'liquid' into the line.
T 'When we came back from play what had happened to the chocolate?'
C5 'It had gone cold.'
C5 then placed 'cold' in the line.
T 'What did it feel like?'
C6 'It was cold and hard.'
C6 put 'hard' into the line.
T 'We have used nearly all our cards but there is one left. It is 'reversible'. What does 'reversible' mean. When have you heard this word before?'

The children then talked for a minute with their talk partner. Some children decided that cars did this and lorries too. With some questioning the direction was obtained – that it was going backwards.

T 'In science when something goes back to what it was before it is said to be a reversible change.'
T 'Can we use reversible in our word line?'
C7 'Yes, the chocolate is reversible.'
T 'Good, melting chocolate is a change that goes back so it is reversible. The change is reversible.'
T 'So what does heat do to chocolate?'
Chn 'It makes it melt.'

The chain of cards read 'solid', 'hot', 'melted', 'liquid', 'cold', 'hard', 'solid', and 'reversible'. This chain of words was then used for butter and lard with different children.

The case study above shows that children can use words, that it is important that key words are selected, and although 'melting' is a process word, it is one used day to day (for instance, 'ice cream melts') so it is not totally new to learners. Using different substances one at a time, starting with chocolate, the one with the highest registration for the learners, butter and jelly were then used to aid the reinforcement of language.

Repetition is vital if learners are to retain language. Having key words for each science topic ensures the focus is clear and the number used in the case study ensured the short-term memory was not over-loaded (the seven, plus or minus two rule (Miller, 1956) introduced earlier in the book). Learners are also more likely to be given reinforcement in a number of different settings if the vocabulary is not too extensive to begin with. Unless children use language in context and actually see it, they are unlikely to be able to make the link between their practical tasks and learning. After making a word sentence the Year 2 children in the case study drew pictures and added words; all of them used at least three of the words in their work. Many used all of the words and they continued to use word cards and modelled language throughout their work in this topic.

3 Learners need to be given help to extend their word understanding and word usage.

Providing learners with their own science dictionaries, like a simple spelling book to store the words they are introduced to, is a very effective way of developing independent learners. Providing picture cards with words underneath them is helpful for less literate learners, as these will also give visual clues for the language. When sharing success criteria, making science vocabulary a central point of attention (for example, 'I can use at least three of the science words in my work') can help to focus learners' attention on the words they use. Older learners may enjoy finding out why some science words are used and can try tracing their usage from the Greeks or Romans.

ICT   One excellent use of interactive whiteboards is to store word maps from one lesson to the next. This ensures that each lesson can start with the words used in the previous one. With older learners additional words can be added as lessons progress.

4 Reinforcing language continually

Playing games is a good way to reinforce the learning of science vocabulary, because it gives variety to lesson structures and this will help learners remember the varying content. The element of fun and the competition also motivate learners including those who would suffer from non-consideration if the learning were in a different format. Here there is only space enough to introduce a few language games (some of which have been mentioned in Chapter 2) as a method for reinforcing and retaining memory.

Bingo

It is useful to play science word bingo. Here the teacher has the definitions and the learners have cards with key science words on them. They have to work out the word that the teacher is defining, and if they have that word on their card they cover it with a counter. The winner could be the pair of learners able to cover all their words first (or just a line if time is limited).

Pairs and chains

Matching pairs is a fun and easy way of enabling learners to link key words with their meanings. Before beginning it is useful to have some that can be used as examples. Chain games (where the card is split into two with a question and answer) are also a simple, interesting way to develop vocabulary (see Figure 5.1). The idea here is to see how long it takes to complete a chain and then to challenge the group to improve on the time next time the game is played. This will help learners not only to decode the word but also acts as a reminder of its meaning.

Games are a good way to develop language as learners are using the words in an everyday setting and there are opportunities for repetition.

Key Stage 2 materials and their properties: Chain/link game

Thermal insulator	Materials that will not let light pass through them		Opaque	A physical change is also called		A reversible change	Water boils at

100 degrees	Like magnetic poles		Repel	Liquid formed by melting ice		Water	Material that does conduct heat

Figure 5.1 A chain game

Teachers should model vocabulary and use the correct language in all activities. Learners find some concepts like dissolving and melting difficult to distinguish between and often use words inappropriately. As far as they are concerned both processes start with solids, end with liquids and heat is sometimes a common factor. No wonder it is hard for them to understand!

This is where a concept chain is useful so that teaching focuses clearly on the important points in a way that learners can understand. Therefore in melting, there is only one substance (ice cream, chocolate, butter and so on) and it changes its state from solid to liquid. When things dissolve there are two materials, the solute and the solvent, which make the solution. Promoting learners to develop understanding and thereby make more links is important and providing them with simple comparisons will help here. As discussed earlier in the book, it is the forging of links that helps understanding.

Such comparisons could be, 'What are the differences between …'

- dissolving and melting?
- a stem and a skeleton?
- pitch and loudness?

Some points to think about

Scientific vocabulary should be developed as an ongoing element within a lesson and not as the focus for the whole lesson. There needs to be context and meaning if any understanding of words is to be retained. It is better not to have this as a learning intention, although it is helpful to have scientific vocabulary as the success criteria that learners understand and work towards.

When new vocabulary is being introduced add a few words at a time. If textbooks and photocopied sheets are part of this it is important to ensure that they do not contain too many new words that learners have not met before. While such activities might have a limited role in learning they are not a substitute for active involvement.

Monitoring the development of language

If learners are asked to make a mind map of the words they know at the start of a topic, it is possible to compare this with the words expected (or that will be needed) in the forthcoming work. These can be used to identify which new words should be introduced and those that will need to be assessed to ensure relevant understanding. The mind map can be used at the end of a topic when learners can add any words and understanding they have gained through the work.

For example, Leila (Year 6) showed she knew eight things about plants at the start of her topic (see Figure 5.2). There was some subject-specific vocabulary, for instance, roots, leaves and flowers. These are low level for her age (Level 2). There was also higher knowledge about breathing, and the role of the leaf and she understood that plants need water and are living things.

By the end of the topic (see Figure 5.3) it is not just the increase in the number of things known (now 12) but also the quality of her ideas that matter. Many indicate a more complex understanding at the

Green plants

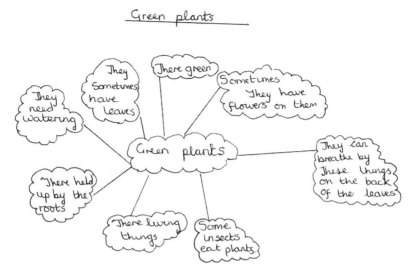

Figure 5.2 Plants pre-teaching

Figure 5.3 Plants post-teaching

expectation for Level 1. She still, however, has some misconceptions that are focused on the use of key words, for example 'the plant drinks water'.

It is through an active learner's involvement in activities ensuring repetition, retention and retrieval that knowledge and understanding are retained and can be drawn upon long after the end of the topic.

(The use of mind maps to support assessment is developed further in Chapter 7.)

Talk About Cards

When discussing science, reinforcing key issues – such as animals are not just pets and fish, birds and humans are also animals – is vitally important. Talk About Cards targets the problematic aspects of science and uses common misconceptions to develop language and learning. Learners are confronted with statements and questions to think about and respond to, for example:

> 'Sarah thought that "volume" was a word to describe how loud sound is. What do you think?'
> 'Would all scientists agree that "diet" is when people try to lose weight and involves not eating chocolate?'

The issue of words having two meanings, one in everyday use and another within scientific language, is something that will always be present. Identifying key words that cause problems and introducing them into the teaching programme for discussion will enable learners to develop an understanding that science is about the world and they can understand and use words to explain its concepts and events.

Summary

Learners need to use language in context. They need to be active in their learning in order to build links and pathways within the brain. Isolated lists of words have no meaning for most learners as they do not have the long-term memory traces to make sense of them. Games will help make learning of vocabulary and associated concepts fun and this might engage and motivate those who have decided science is not for them. It is important that the four simple rules of language development (discussed above) are considered if learners are to be scientifically literate. This is significant because all adults need to be aware of global issues, even if they do not work in the field of science.

Putting this into practice

- Model simple scientific vocabulary throughout the topic; if words are used in context learners will be more likely to use them.
- Ensure the scientific vocabulary of complex concepts is not being used before the concept is understood; for example gravity, evaporation or dissolving. Develop understanding using everyday language first.
- Use active learning approaches to promote the development of vocabulary, e.g. games, key words, bingo.
- Use free range concept maps, or mind maps, to help promote and monitor learners' developing vocabulary development.
- Identify key words and identify those whose everyday meaning is different from that in science.

6

How to write in science

This chapter will focus on the various genres of science writing, the importance of promoting learners' ability to communicate their understanding and how this improves thinking. A range of different strategies to enable learners to demonstrate what they know will be developed. These will not focus on what can be copied from the board after a shared discussion! Although the modelling of writing is a key feature in learning how to write, copying does not develop a learner's ability to think. Approaches will be developed alongside examples of learners' work. Some current classroom practices that are effective in developing scientific writing will be explored from a brain-based learning perspective. These include, 'floor books', the use of digital cameras to promote learning and interactive logbooks.

Historical reasons for current practice

There is a key need to develop different ways for learners to demonstrate their knowledge. Many published worksheets are not suitable for whole-class work as they provide no meaningful opportunities to extend the more able, who may resort to colouring in pictures when they have finished their tasks, nor do they support the least able who often have problems reading the task and as a result have little understanding of what they are doing. There is also a concern that relates to how many learners actually 'do the work'. Observations have shown that many learners copy from each other. The only time this becomes apparent to a teacher is when there is a misunderstanding and a spate of wrong answers emerges throughout a group.

One of the advantages of being older is having taught prior to the advent of new technology. In the early 1980s there were few photocopiers in British schools, only Banda machines, and these required teachers to create their own materials. The smell of spirit and indelible ink is an early teaching memory! The introduction of the photocopier and published materials provided welcome support for busy teachers when the National Curriculum was introduced. At the time such materials appeared to provide suitable resources for both teachers and learners.

However, in this case perhaps this was an example of behaviour growing better before it grows worse (Senge, 1990). The solutions appear to improve matters when in reality they are creating different, and often greater, long-term problems. Schools now spend a considerable portion of their budgets on photocopying materials and this is often at the expense of resources for practical science. The overall cost is causing some institutions to review this practice, but from a budget rather than from a teaching and learning perspective. Some are replacing this technology with a focus on e-learning.

The use of new approaches needs to be planned for carefully because in themselves they will not necessarily promote a better development of learning in science, and especially recording, any more than the methods they replace. There is a need to change habits and look to different approaches both for learners and teachers, so that learners are using their brains more.

In the pursuit of evidence

The other issue that prevents learners from systematically developing their ability to record outcomes from science learning is a perceived need for subjects and schools to hold evidence for scrutiny and inspection. There has been an overwhelming influence through recent educational culture for schools to demonstrate accountability and in doing so to have masses of supportive paperwork in the form of policies, planning and hard evidence of learning. This has largely been seen as 'stuff' in learners' books! The measure of accountability is changing and schools are having to demonstrate through self-evaluation a capacity to identify both what they need to improve and how they will make this happen. Unfortunately in some schools this change of focus has had little impact on the requirement for teachers to produce quantities of 'hard' evidence of teaching and much time is still spent on both photocopying and ensuring these sheets get into books.

The resulting activities are not likely to be memorable or motivating for learners as they are all too similar in format and it is known that things which are similar are less likely to be remembered. Also the stimuli are not very great, so it is less likely this learning will be added to the long-term memory. Many learners undertake a diet of so-called 'flat work' or 'seat work', that is then supplemented by a discussion that is summarised in written form on the board by the teacher and then copied into books by learners. The reason for this approach which is given by many teachers is that most learners may not write very much if left to their own devices. This vicious circle then continues as children progress through school and results in learners in Year 6 who find writing and explaining their ideas in science very hard. Such issues are identified in national evaluations of learning. Recently it was suggested that to improve performance pupils need to be given opportunities to

> write their own conclusions to investigations and discuss what makes a good conclusion. (QCA, 2006: 2)

A key issue raised by Lyotard (1984), which will inform the rest of this chapter, is whether all success should be judged against the ability to save time because 'thinking has a fatal flaw; it wastes time' (p. 122). Thinking is time consuming and therefore not a very modern commodity when all devices are favoured for their timesaving nature! Being able to express one's thoughts in a way that can clearly be communicated to others takes even more time and involves some basic skills. Published science has its own genre and this can make recording ideas confusing for younger learners who are expected to adopt this style. Linking the written and spoken language of science is as important as the integration of reading and writing in Literacy. The writing conventions used in science might at times be different from story writing, although there are examples when the use of a story genre can support the development of ideas, which is the important part of science (see Figure 6.1).

The myth of science

In teaching science there are a number of myths and one of these is that science is about doing and not writing. The doing is important, but so too is recording outcomes. Another myth lies in the genre of writing in science; method, apparatus, results and conclusions should always be used. Scientists do have a set way of working when they publish their work. All reports are published in an accepted format and even educational research is published in an agreed form. Most authors, even famous ones like JK Rowling, will not suggest they get

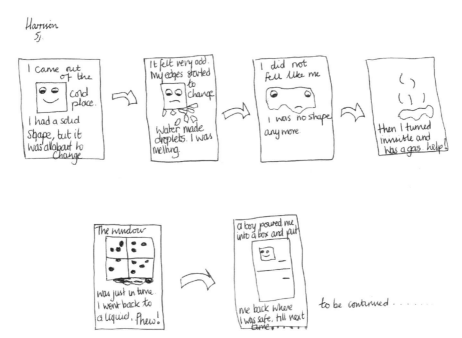

Figure 6.1 Harrison's work

it right first time and it goes straight from brain to published work in one attempt. Note taking, scribbles, jotting, charts and diagrams that illustrate the development of ideas and thoughts all play an important part in the process. Learners need to be given a chance to develop their science writing. It is well known that some learners, who have considerable prior knowledge and are skilled at writing, find it useful to write in more than one format and will have several attempts to achieve an end point. Perhaps younger learners with less experience should also be given such opportunities. On a 'Scientist write' website, the following comments were found:

ICT

> if you can't communicate that to others, your value to an organisation is limited. Put it another way – you won't find too many engineering jobs that only require you to sit in a room by yourself designing and building things. Write a little everyday and be accountable to others, you will write more. (http://scientistswrite.blogspot.com)

Scientists write in order to share their ideas and the sharing and publication of their work are important aspects of the developmental process. Without the sharing of ideas, science as a body of knowledge, understanding and skills does not move forward and the world is less well off. On an individual level, sharing ideas and thoughts strengthens the links in the brain and as a result more learning can occur. Not everyone likes to write and even Darwin is suggested to have said 'a naturalist's life would be a happy one if he had only to observe and never to write'. His notebooks were full of drawings, pictures, thoughts and sketches. Without his commitment to communicate these ideas to others his viewpoint on evolution might not have been widely understood. Some scientists think that his theory of evolution was a key feature of science in the twentieth century. Without evolution and evolutionary theory, recent developments in medicine or farming that are extending human life and helping to prevent people from starving may not have taken place.

> Few other ideas in science have had such a far-reaching impact on our thinking about ourselves and how we relate to the world. (NAS, 1998: 21)

One question to ponder could be how many new ideas would not have been developed or understood if Darwin had merely observed but not recorded! Some of the greatest scientists, Newton and Einstein for example, were not skilled in writing when they were children. However, unlike some less literate learners of today they did not regard themselves as failures. There is a place for developing the range of science writing that learners are involved with. This needs to begin with emergent science writing that will be continually developed throughout schooling.

Key features of developing science writing

Recording in science is an area where teachers worry most, yet by using learning to adopt relevant strategies learners and teachers can be supported. There is no quick fix but quick fixes are not effective in the long term anyway. There are four key features to improving science writing.

1 All who are involved in writing in science must perceive that it has value.
2 A range of opportunities is provided.
3 Science writing has meaning and occurs when learners want to record their thoughts, ideas and so on at the same time as engaging in practical tasks.
4 It should provide a record that could be the subject of further discussion and evaluation.

1 Science writing has value

Written work in science has value if it has a high profile and status. Sharing outcomes by displaying work gives learners a sense of value. Placing samples of individuals' work in a class logbook demonstrates it is valued. Changing the format, length and type of recording shows an interest in the learners. Allowing learners a choice in the methods and/or genre they can select, and by making it part of the science experience, shows that 'mark making', in whatever form, is part of science and is worthwhile.

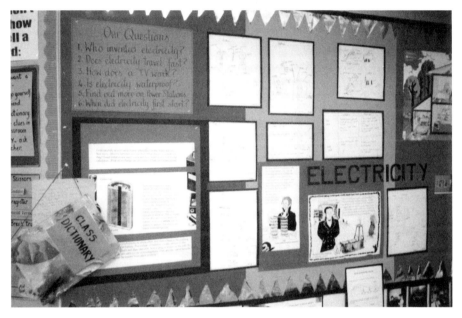

Figure 6.2 A photograph of a display – valuing science and science writing

The work shown in Figure 6.2 exemplifies the value of science by including learners' work, their questions, and writing from other sources.

2 Different opportunities

In order to make learning meaningful it has to be registered by the brain and in order to be retained and retrieved later it must be undertaken in a way that will make gestalts form. If learning is too similar it will be forgotten. To help make learning memorable a range of opportunities for undertaking science writing should be provided, for example, by labelling materials with Post-it notes. Using Post-it notes, young children can observe and label the objects in the classroom that are for instance made of everyday materials. A teacher might select the material (say, wood) for a child or group of children to identify and label. This allows learners to develop vocabulary; it is movement orientated and as a result more links are made with the brain. It is different from 'seat work', the stimulus is higher and the task likely to

ICT   motivate. The teacher can ask a learner to take a photograph using a digital camera as a record. The labels can later be removed which allows reinforcement. A teacher can see if learners understand this key feature of science by discerning where they place the Post-it notes. Discussion can occur later using the photograph and if this is put onto an electronic logbook some typed words could also be added. The task can be differentiated by giving more or less Post-it notes to some learners or by changing the type of materials selected, for example, identifying objects which are made both of wood and of metal. Laminated shaped cards are useful for beginning writers as they are bigger, allowing more room for words.

It is also important for learners to see writing in science. Games, where words and pictures are matched, provide a stimulus for seeing science writing in a fun context (see Chapter 5). If some pictures are provided but the words are missing learners can write their own labels to develop this understanding further. Even simple writing in wet sand can help develop confidence in science writing and the texture of the sand provides a different stimulus, again reinforcing learning. All these approaches will help develop links and are easy and of a short duration.

3 Learners need to see science writing as being meaningful

Learners need to see that their writing in science has a purpose and the time spent on it is worthwhile. If they feel that the time spent is wasted because the work is going into their books never to be looked at again then there will be little or no arousal. Recording in the class logbook or scrapbook, however, provides a special value and meaning for their work. Selecting two learners to record in the scrapbook each session can supply a varied record of their science over time. This approach provides recorded evidence of the science that has been undertaken as well as a demonstration of a range of alternative methods to record outcomes. This class book or scrapbook also allows learners to refer back to the activities they have taken part in and to retrieve learning at a later time.

Evidence has shown that if pictures and drawings by classes are included in these books learners will use them frequently because they like to look back and refresh their memory about the things they have done. In one class a simple diary was used to encourage daily recording of what was occurring, for example, with butterflies, tadpoles, snails, seeds or the environment the class was observing. Everyone in the class enjoyed the book, as it contained their writing, pictures and thoughts. Learners will also be more motivated if they understand that formal recordings will be used to aid discussions in the future about the ideas held and conclusions reached. To support those with less literacy skills the adults in the class can initially record learners' ideas in speech bubbles.

Whenever possible, opportunities should be found to 'mark make'. There should be a wide range of formats and the learner should not feel under pressure to get it right first time. Whiteboards, Post-it notes and talking postcards all provide such opportunities. Talking postcards will allow a few spoken sentences to be recorded because they contain a small voice recording chip and an erase feature. The front is also suitable for writing on with a dry-wipe pen. They allow a learner to store writing and a picture of an object, as well as their voice. As they also come with a plastic cover, a permanent record of a favourite object or photograph can be kept. They can be used again and again and will help support emergent science writing.

ICT

It is important to give children the chance to 'make marks' in every science lesson. This does not have to be a large quantity of written work and to be successful the type of recording should vary and not focus purely on writing words. Learners need to be encouraged by the teacher that this is what is expected. They need to know that drawings, words and notes help scientists to remember something important while they work. To support this it is vital that paper, whiteboards, markers and crayons are available for younger children. Older learners should benefit from having access to their own science notebooks.

4 It provides opportunities for further discussion

As understanding and learning are the focus for recording in science, it is important to encourage drawings, cartoons, notes and simple diagrams, as well as longer pieces of work. When learners write (or scribble) a teacher should frequently encourage them to read what they have produced back to them as this provides information about the

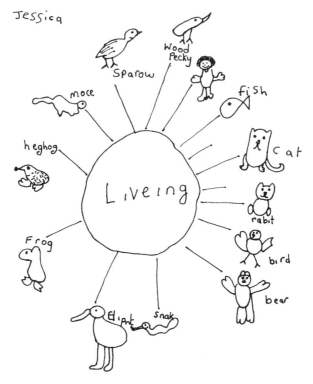

**Figure 6.3 An early opportunity to record an understanding of living things –
this Year 1 child shows an understanding of animals being alive but not
plants (the child enjoyed the task and did not see it as work)**

learners' prior understanding as well as the links they are making with
their current learning. At times it is also useful to scribe their point of
view so it can be shared again later. This is useful for the most able
older learners as well as the least literate four year-olds because it
adds to their understanding and is a more permanent record than conversation. Such activities uncover relevant questions that will help
move understanding forward. Such opportunities are rare when learners fill in a worksheet. Some examples of scribed discussion on learners' work showing ideas are illustrated by Figures 6.4 and 6.5.

In Figure 6.4 the learner's understanding is demonstrated by a
series of drawings. The scribing shows the learner understands why
some things live in some places (Year 2). The quality of the drawing
for a six year-old is good, but their understanding of animals shows
knowledge. Because it took about half an hour to complete the
activity, this provided time for links to be made in the brain, in a way
that a worksheet completed in five minutes would not.

tropical rainforest part of it is cold and part is hot so they have warmth and cold so it is just right.
Special spider
trap
Web
he eats them
Lion he is free in the forest. Nice and damp and hot.
toads live in ponds because they have skin that would peel off if it got dry
fly
toad
Lizards
he is cam himself
He lives in the rainforest
He needs hot and damp.
Fly trap
plant that lives in the rainforest It is hot and animals won't expect a live plant there. The fly goes for the honey and the mouth will shut.
Catcus
Need heat because they have to have heat to make the prickles.
They don't need water because they have water inside
The prickles are made out of stone... I don't know what they are made of
Beavers make dams. Have lots of water
trap the fish and build the huts

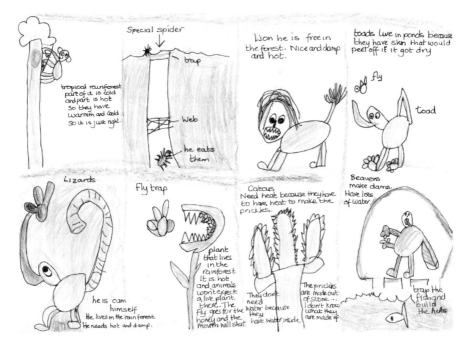

Figure 6.4 Where things live and why

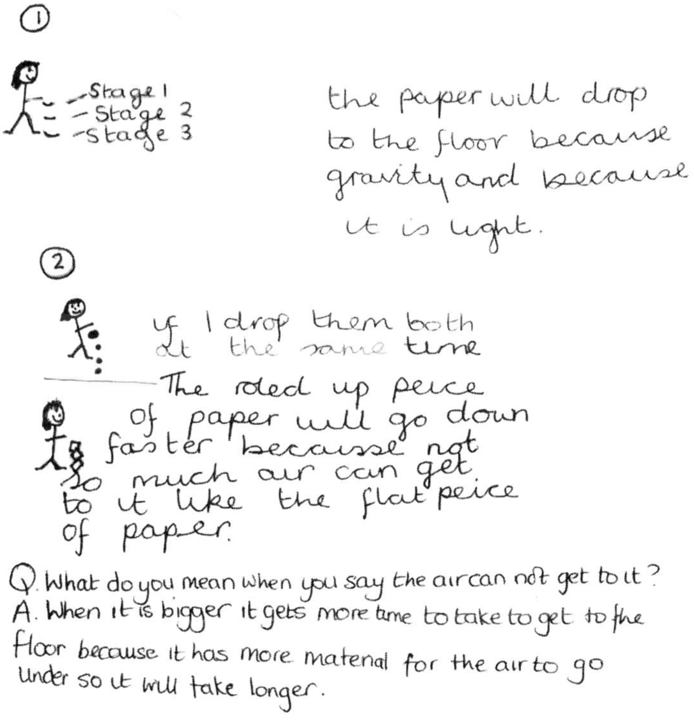

1
Stage 1
Stage 2
Stage 3
the paper will drop to the floor because gravity and because it is light.
2
if I drop them both at the same time
The roled up peice of paper will go down faster becausse not so much air can get to it like the flat peice of paper.
Q. What do you mean when you say the air can not get to it?
A. When it is bigger it gets more time to take to get to the floor because it has more material for the air to go under so it will take longer.

Figure 6.5 Ideas about gravity and recorded discussion

In the case of Figure 6.5 the teacher recorded a discussion, about gravity and air resistance, with a Year 5 girl. This provides opportunities for both parties to look back at the work and the learner's ideas at a future time. It also demonstrated that the ideas were worthy of being written down.

Floor books

Floor books have been used in primary education for about a decade, but have not been as well used as other strategies for recording science. The National Curriculum In Action website (www. ncaction.org.uk/search/index.htm) has an example of a floor book from 2000. The work records an investigation from a Year 1 class on how to stop an apple from going brown. Floor books are useful in that they provide a record of learners' ideas and, because of the value attached to them, they can motivate children to become involved in an activity. Whilst some teachers build up a floor book over a series of lessons, others complete the work in only one. The link with the brain will be more effective if the memory traces are left to develop and learners will also sometimes change their ideas when they have time to reflect. Older learners can work in groups on their own big books. Floor books, like any type of recording, are more useful if learners can see a use for them, for example to report to other classes if there is more than one class of the same age group in the school, or to share their results with younger children. When learners see relevance and value in activities their arousal is greater also.

Drawing and sequence drawings

Although learners can often draw before they can write, not all learners will have exceptional drawing skills and this should not matter. Learners will develop skills if they feel encouraged and that it is safe to do so. Learners with low self-esteem, or those who are 'labelled' as bright and therefore feel they have to live up to this accolade, can spend too much time rubbing out their ideas. Every learner needs to know that it will not matter if it is not perfect first time round. To enable these drawings to provide insight into learners' thinking, and to help children develop as science writers, some words are usually needed. A key issue here seems to be the lack of writing skills that enable learners to capture their thoughts and ICT thus add them to their pictures. Providing learners with a sheet of sticky labels, each pre-prepared with key words, can help them to start to annotate their drawings. This scaffolding technique has been found to be successful in promoting eventual independence. If learners are never given these opportunities they will never get started. It is useful here to return to the ideas of Senge (1990).

ICT

Remember the 'Take two aspirin and wait' rule

Most people know that it is necessary to wait patiently for aspirins to take effect because aspirin works with a delay. Using this analogy, the delay in getting better at writing might take a few months, but without a concerted effort and a common approach in school to 'mark making' in science no improvement will be seen. It will get messy before it gets better. Handwriting practice from the board does not require learners to think, only copy. When learners have to think for themselves presentation usually deteriorates for a short time.

Without the ability to record there is no opening to share ideas and thoughts, thus reducing the interaction of ideas. Drawings help to give focus and teachers can use these to develop an understanding of the development of learning. Learners can look at each other's work and see where they are the same and where they differ. As their confidence develops, their ability to record their ideas will improve. The fact that they record in their own way is more meaningful to them and more meaningful experiences are remembered. Without 'mark making' there is little focus on skill development in the individual.

ICT

Digital cameras are used regularly in schools for taking pictures of learners involved in investigative work. These are printed and stuck into books to record the science that occurred. However, digital camera pictures can also be downloaded onto sticky address labels (those used for addressing envelopes work well) and as a result a range of stickers can be produced to support recording.

Recording by drawing helps to provide a focus for learners' ideas. There is a theory here that learners should write first and illustrate later, as they might just draw the pictures and then never get around to doing any writing. If word cards are provided along with dictionaries of words or a science sheet of common words with pictures attached, learners are supported and can record independently. There are many situations where it is worthwhile to do the drawings first, in order to see or visualise what they are about to do.

CASE STUDY

A class of six-year-old learners was playing with musical instruments and seeing how to use them to make noise. They talked about instruments that have to be hit and those that could be blown. They sorted the instruments and put them into groups. The teacher knew some learners would not be able to write the names of the instruments, or draw them in a way that they could recognise later, so she took pictures of the instruments and turned these into stickers. After the children had explored and sorted the instruments, she gave them some picture stickers and asked them to put them into their books to record their ideas. She talked to them about how they could use the stickers, by putting them in groups or making marks on them, like B for blow, H for hit. She then allowed the children to stick the pictures into their books by themselves how they wanted. She had also provided some word cards for more able children to allow them to record words as well if they liked.

All the children completed the sticking as a bare minimum, and were able to talk about how sound was made. Although it takes time to photograph the instruments, once they are prepared they can be used time and again. Some more able children recorded their musical instruments in the form of a table, so differentiation through outcome was demonstrated.

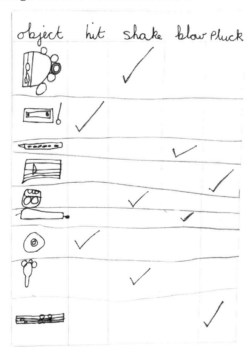

Figure 6.6 Musical instruments make sounds

In Figure 6.6 the child designed the table and recorded how the sound was produced, and the instruments were drawn as well. All pupils recorded in their own way even though they were only six years old, as they had developed the confidence to do so.

Drawing what you need to use

When planning an investigation it is vital that the children are asked to draw all the things (equipment) they will need to use in their investigation. The following examples (Figures 6.7 to 6.10) show that learners will know what equipment they will need. They display what will be measured and what factors they are changing. This helps learners to use images, which again builds networks in the brain. The Greeks were right!

Figure 6.7 A year 6 child's recording of his plan

Here the child's work shows his plan for a spinner investigation. He was changing the height and measuring the spins. The health and safety issue was discussed and he therefore used a PE box to stand on and not a chair. This child had a statement for lack of literacy. This was the first completed work he produced unaided in science.

Figure 6.8 A table to record results

Stephen then showed his result (Figure 6.8). He was able to understand his own table, a new experience for him, because it made sense
and he understood what it was for. Allowing learners to make their
records personal helps to make them more meaningful. Meaning is
needed for understanding.

Figure 6.9 A Key Stage 1 picture plan: which ball will bounce the highest?

Figure 6.9 shows that even learners under the age of seven can visualise what they will do and what they will need. This prevents a classroom full of unsure learners and the teacher, by looking at the
pictures, will know if anyone needs further support.

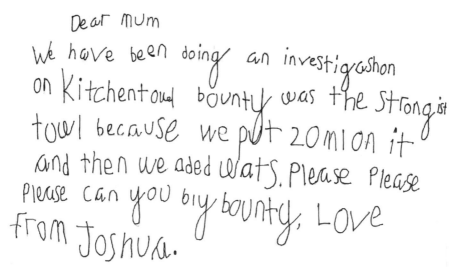

Dear mum

We have been doing an investigashon on kitchentowl bounty was the strongist towl because we put 20ml on it and then we aded wats. Please Please Please can you biy bounty, Love from Joshua.

**Figure 6.10 A letter to Mummy. Here Joshua reports back to his Mum,
requesting that she buys Bounty paper towels when she goes shopping!**

The learners in the examples shown were able to demonstrate what
they were changing, what they were measuring and also had
opportunities to think through their investigation by planning it out
in their mind first. This will help with **registration** and it also helps
teachers to assess if learners know what to use and how to make
readings. It also provides a place for recording ideas. If the
recordings occur throughout the lesson and not just at the end, it
ensures learners are thinking and not just doing. Linking both 'hands
on and minds on'! Having to make a record of what they are going
to use and being able to select their equipment increase motivation
and provide a real reason for undertaking the recording exercise. If
recording only happens at the end of the lesson or a future lesson is
devoted to recording what happened last time, the value and use of
recording are not apparent for learners. Indeed they may well think
it is for their teacher and not for them. Similarly, there is a danger
that they will forget what has happened in time. This approach
results in reluctance by even able learners to put pen to paper, as they
see little real reason to undertake the task.

Figure 6.11 Speech writing (Year 2)

At the end of an investigation it is important to find out what learners have understood. Talking to each one is time consuming and a classroom 'chat' often only involves a few learners. Using speech writing for the results makes it fun (Figure 6.11). In all the classes where this has been tried it has resulted in more marks being made. It is important to get some written work from young children as 'the early childhood years – from birth through to age eight, are considered the most important period for literacy development' (NAEYC, 2003).

Written work can be supported with the use of a word wall. If a word wall is created and key words and sentences are used, along with pictures, it provides a stimulating environment for developing language. When words are used in class time by referring back to the wall, this helps to support learning. Learners should be encouraged to add words and phrases as well. The word wall should change with varying themes and topics in science. Having to get up and move to look at words also helps with independence and brain learning. Filling part of the class with bright visual science stimuli and having learners make posters, word mobiles and diagrams will support their understanding and provide an audience for their work (see Chapter 8).

ICT Learners can share their science investigations in a children's science website. One of the best sites is Sci-Journal supported by Patrick Fullick at the University of Southampton. This site has been running for a number of years and is well organised, modern and supports children and teachers (www.sci-journal.org/).

ICT Learners can share work, by email, with other learners at neighbouring schools and thus another audience is created. Making an e-journal that records the results of all work undertaken by learners in science is also very effective. Some work can be scanned, some articles written online and pictures from the digital camera can all be added and used to support science development. Again the learner's work is valued – it has a real audience and also provides evidence that will positively support school self-evaluation. Additionally and more importantly learners can access their work again and again, which fosters further understanding of the content as well as supporting the **retention** and **retrieval** of the information covered. This work has to be organised by a teacher to ensure that key events are included and that all work in a topic area is kept together, as together this will help with chunking.

Poems and rhymes, stories, cartoon strips and word trees all help learners to record science in different ways. Ensuring that the greatest number of ways possible are provided will result in learners having the biggest opportunity to develop all aspects of emergent science writing. It will also ensure the optimum amount of links are made, which will enhance retention and retrieval.

Summary

Effective learning takes time, and recording might develop slowly. If learners are encouraged to 'mark make' alongside any practical work in science, and not after the fun occurs, they will see reasons and have the motivation to complete the task. Any genre is appropriate for writing in science and more formal ways of recording can be introduced at a later stage. Once understanding and confidence have been developed both by teachers and learners, new and interesting ways of recording can be discovered and will be adopted. For example, making a model of a plant and including all the parts of the flower is an excellent way to record key features and to learn about stamens, stigma and styles. Marks do not only have to be made on paper! Such activities make learning fun but are harder to accomplish than merely labelling a sheet. However, because arousal is likely to be high and various senses are being used, the activity and the learning that accompanies it are likely to remain in the memory, especially if the learners themselves invent the plant and flower. Taking photos provides clues, cues and memory traces. It also enables creativity, and this will be developed further in Chapter 8. Writing in science is valuable and teaching learners to be science writers requires discipline and routine – without this everyone suffers needlessly (Senge, 1990)!

Putting this into practice
- Allow learners to record things in many different ways, and to have choice in the methods of recording.
- Do not be upset or panic when presentation dips whilst learners are focusing on the content and not just the handwriting.
- Real learning takes time and recording should occur throughout the lesson and not only at the end, or worse as a lesson on its own!
- Science is about communicating understanding, and drawings, pictures, cartoons, speech and so on are as vital as the 'hands-on' aspects of the lesson because without these opportunities meaning is not made by learners.
- ICT can aid recording, and digital cameras, email and electronic scrapbooks are all useful tools to support learners in using their brains.

7

Assessment in science

This chapter will discuss how formative assessment can develop thinking skills and promote attainment. Reference will be made to examples of effective feedback and the use of assessment levels to inform planning and target setting. While formative assessment is known to be a powerful tool for improving learning, with registered gains that are the equivalent of moving a medium-ranked country on the TIMS test to one of the top 5,[1] it is not a set of strategies that can just be added to everyday teaching. In order for such gains to be achieved there has to be a fundamental change in the contract between teachers and learners and a focus on how learners' brains work.

Sharing learning intentions, improved questioning and feedback marking are often quoted as the key aspects of formative assessment. It is true that these are useful strategies, however without empowering learners and taking action as a result of assessment information there will be little impact on their progress. It is also important to make the link back to how children learn, because whilst formative assessment is powerful, its impact is being limited and is less than it should be (Deforges, 2006; Black, 2007).

The impact of testing on teaching

The testing culture and the standards agenda that followed the introduction of the National Curriculum have had an impact on teaching and learning.

---

[1] Dylan Wiliam (1999) and also http://www.pdkintl.org/kappan/kbla9810.htm

> Ofsted is concerned that some teachers are narrowing the curriculum during the last year of primary school to focus on SATs revision. Schools report that they feel pressured to focus on SATs to help pupils get good results; to ensure a good Ofsted report; and to get a good position in the school league tables. (Parliamentary Office of Science and Technology Primary Report, 2003: 3)

This impact is not unique to the British system. The annual testing system in the USA has also raised questions about whether it is valuable to learners.

> Again, to be sure, accurate scores are essential. But there remains an unasked prior question: How can we maximize the positive impact of our scores on learners? Put another way, how can we be sure that our assessment instruments, procedures, and scores serve to help learners want to learn and feel able to learn? (Stiggins, 2002: 760)

The debates about education and the impact of tests and testing are found not only across the USA but also in Australia as well as much of Europe. Interestingly the push for performance is as common as the worry about learners who leave school unable to read and write.

> international studies show that 30 per cent of 15 year olds in Australia do not have the literacy and numeracy skills which will enable them to hold down a meaningful job in the future or undertake life-long learning. (Cassidy, 2006)

The introduction of the National Curriculum and testing was to ensure that the standards would rise and there would be no underachievement. Pollard (1992) suggested that only the standards that could be raised were those on flagpoles and the focus on standards would not be in the interests of learners, but this viewpoint and concern did not catch the attention of the teaching population. Perhaps as schools struggled with implementing a National Curriculum time was not left for additional debate. It was only in the late 1990s that the wider issues associated with assessment and learning came to popular attention when Black and Wiliam (1989a)[2] reported on the role of formative assessment. When a summary of key findings was published in a pamphlet called 'Inside the Black Box' (Black and Wiliam, 1989b), the

---

[2] They initially looked at about 580 articles and chapters to see if formative assessment would raise standards, focusing on 250 published articles and chapters from a range of sources, with funding from the Nuffield Foundation, in a study commissioned by the Assessment Reform Group, with their findings published in an educational research journal.

formative assessment phenomenon was born. Even Black and Wiliam acknowledge the impact of 'inside the black box':

> In some respects, 'inside the black box' represented our opinions and prejudices as much as anything else, although we would like to think that these are supported by evidence, and are consistent with the 50 years of experience in this field that we had between us. It is also important to note that the success of 'inside the black box' has been as much due to its rhetorical force as to its basis in evidence. (Black and Wiliam, 2005: 226)

The term Assessment for Learning (AFL) was coined by the Assessment Reform Group (ARG) a year later. It was the ARG that originally commissioned Black and Wiliam's review of the research. Black and Wiliam continued to state that AFL was not a 'magic formula' and there were no quick fixes. Indeed, the findings from the Kings, Medway and Oxford Formative Assessment Project (KMOFAP) (Black and Wiliam, 2001) illustrate these points, as changes in classroom practice were very personal to the teachers involved and by no means standard. Nevertheless, the possibility of improving performance has resulted in A4L becoming a strand in both the National Secondary and National Primary strategies and is promoted by most local authorities. However, in many schools there has been a form of 'cherry picking' from the ten principles of AFL. Most schools will now demonstrate lessons with learning objectives that are shared with learners, and will have identified outcomes of learning. Some have clear success criteria and even share these with learners. The key aspect of AFL, the involvement of both teacher and learner in making change actions by using information from assessment, is much less evident. Where it is, however, the roles of teacher and learner are radically different; the learner is a partner in the process and is expected to use their brain!

A key outcome of the KMOFAP project was the recognition that for learning to improve there had to be a change in teaching styles and that learning is not something you can do to or for someone.

> It became clear to the teachers that, no matter what the pressure to achieve good test and examination scores, learning cannot be done for the student; it has to be done by the student. (Black and Wiliam, 2005: 232)

The reconstruction of the teaching contract is more than just putting the learning intention on the board; this is not assessment for learning. Neither are other individual practices such as talk partners, traffic lights, and peer or comment marking. All of these can be effective in moving learning forward, but the focus must be on learners and how they learn. If the focus is still on the teacher and the strategy and not on learners the outcome is assessment for teaching (Sutton, 2006),[3] not assessment for learning. This was shown recently with a feedback-marking project in Wales. The original research on feedback marking by Butler (1988) quoted in Black and Wiliam (1998a) showed that those students who were not given grades but feedback on their work progressed far more than those given only grades or grades and comments. The latest research reported that a group with only feedback did not do better and in fact did less well than groups given grades alone. Among interesting aspects of this research (Smith and Gorard, 2005) are the responses from the learners.

> *Sometimes I get confused with it because some of my comments, well I just don't really get what they mean to say.*

> *Miss, I'd like to know my marks because comments don't tell us much.*
> (Smith and Gorard, 2005a: 5)

It is the quality of feedback, and not just the absence of grades, that is vital. For the learners above, the feedback is not reinforcing the learning and giving guidance on how to improve. The result is demotivated learners who feel disillusioned and who might demonstrate rejection of the subject or display non-consideration. Either will result in fewer links being made in the brain; this is assessment for teaching, with the emphasis on 'doing it' to the learners!

In order for AFL to be successful the teacher must promote self-belief in learners and change their role to one of enabler rather than presenter. This is not an easy process as there are strong belief systems in place, including the assumption that reading grades to a class will motivate all learners to be top, thus focusing on egos not the task! It was thought this approach had died out but it was recently found to be alive and well in at least one grammar school in the largest authority in England. Labelling learners is something that still happens in many schools, and being labelled can last a lifetime. There are still adults who feel they are not good at a subject because of something that happened twenty years before in school.

---

[3] The term was used at the AAIA annual conference by Ruth Sutton, Newcastle-upon-Tyne, September 2006.

Ego or task centred learning

If learning is to be successful the focus should be on the task. What learners understand about a task and how it links to prior learning should help recruit the neurons to assemblies, developing links and pathways. Feedback helps reinforce learning but only if it is focused on the task. If it is focused on the emotions then other neurons become involved; these might influence the pathways and links and interfere with the learning gestalt formation. Emotions are a very powerful force! When there is a focus on ego, there can only be a few winners. With ego involvement learners compare themselves with their peers and any failure damages their self-esteem (Dweck, 1999). In a system that focuses on ego learners are reluctant to take risks, and react badly to new challenges due to the ever-present fear of failure and being compared negatively to others. Maslow (1954, 1970) developed a hierarchy of needs and suggested that the lower level needs had to be met first. Lower needs are centred in the oldest part of the brain. One lower level need is safety. Until learners feel safe then the higher level needs, like cognition or self-actualisation (growth of the brain by making new pathways and links), cannot occur. Ego focused teaching results in learners who do enough to get by and worry about whether they are right to a point where they might not try new things.

A task centred focus, however, relies on a learner understanding the task, and comparing their performance with the outcome of the task. As the outcome is only compared against their own performance, learners are more willing to undertake new challenges and learn from failure. In order for a task centred focus to be effective learners do need to know what they are learning and why they are learning it, and they have to be given feedback as to their progress. This feedback has to identify what is good, why it is good and how improvements can be made in the future. The cornerstone of the assessment for learning research was on the feedback and feed forward, with the focus on neuron assemblies all related to learning. Feedback must be in a format that learners understand or no links can be made.

Sometimes when they write you can't understand their writing. (Smith and Gorard, 2005b: 5)

Marking for improvement

If learners are to undertake more mark making in science then it is vital that they are given feedback they can act on. The Learn Project (Weedon,

Winter and Bradfoot, 2000) showed the difference between the learners' perspective on marking and the teachers'. The table below is adapted from the Learn Project 2000, with additions from Kent learners.

What is written	What the learners think
'Good work'	Why is it good, in what ways?
'Good'	Does not help much, if he liked it he would have told the truth.
'You must try harder', or 'Could do better!'	!!!!!!! This doesn't help.'
'Could be neater'	You get a sticker for hard work, neat writing the date!
'Spellings!'	Which? I don't want to hear that as I already know that.
'Use paragraphs'	I would if I could but I do not know what one is.
✔	Means he probably likes it.
'Try to develop your explanation'	I did my best, how can I make it better?

Focusing on areas where learners have met the success criteria and providing them with feedback about future actions will develop learners' ability to make progress. This progress will be at the level of the individual, so the marking is differentiated. Work from a sound topic is used to demonstrate this. The learners in a Year 4 class were asked to think about all the things they knew about sound. The success criteria were that they would identify sources of sound, by using writing and pictures, and they would try to use science words to describe different sounds. If there was time they could think of questions about sound they would like to answer (an extension activity). Marking for improvement was used, with each learner being given two smiley faces for where work was good and a triangle point showing what they might improve on at the start of the next lesson.

In Figure 7.1 at first glance it seems problematic to mark like this, yet if feedback marking is to be used effectively two areas should be identified for all learners. On closer inspection it is clear that this boy knows about a number of sources of sound, so one smiley can be given for this. He has also identified that there are high and low sounds, although looking at the pictures he really means loud and quiet sounds. The objects in the middle are lorries and their alarms are loud. A second smiley could be given for the puddle picture, where the sound of rain is shown as ripples. This is good observation and could be used later to help this learner understand about sound

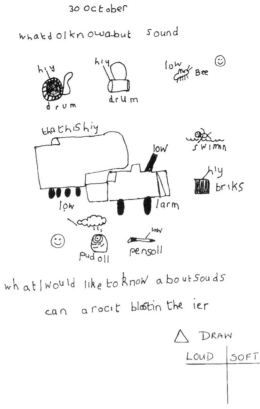

30 October

whatdoIknowabut Sound

hiy

hiy

low   Bee   ☺

drum

drUm

thathishiy

low

swimn

low

hiy   briks

low

larm

low

☺   Pudoll   pensoll

what I would like to know about Souds

can arocit blostin the ier

△ DRAW

LOUD | SOFT

Figure 7.1 Work from a less literate boy from Year 4 who displayed some behaviour issues

traveling, as he already has a mental image to use. His triangle point is to draw pictures of loud and quiet sounds, to see if he can identify different types of sound. It would be pointless to ask this child to write this out, as his skills are not sufficiently developed. It is also important that his self-esteem is enhanced or he will continue to avoid learning and create trouble.

The work in Figure 7.2 could have a number of smileys, but only two can be given otherwise it becomes a competition for the largest number of smileys and does not focus on the work. The most advanced parts of the work were examined and the link between sound traveling distances was one area that was selected here. A second smiley was given to the questions, as this was an extension in the lesson and they are presented clearly. The triangle point was focused on the example of sounds travelling because, although it is a good point, further clarification could have been given by using a different example. This will help this learner to make further links.

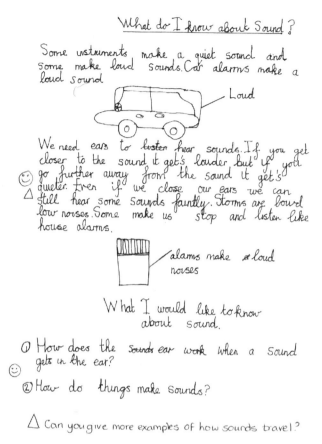

Figure 7.2 Work from a literate girl from Year 4

Marking in this way is transparent and helps all learners move forward, whether they are the brightest in class or someone who has more problems undertaking learning tasks. There is no set or right place to put a smiley; it must be placed where it is most appropriate for that learner. What was found though was that two smileys were more useful, as if only one was given this could limit motivation.

Learners understand their world

Some observers are concerned that teaching in science is more didactic than for other subjects ... It is, however, concerned that the emphasis on literacy and numeracy in recent years has led to a reduction in both the amount of time spent on science and the amount of practical work carried out.(Parliamentary Office of Science and Technology Primary Report, 2003: 3)

A narrowed curriculum focuses too heavily on short-term memory and the learning is often not provided in a way that will enable learners to make links with real life and previous learning. Links are needed if learners are to transfer knowledge to new situations. What is often found is that some learners revert to what they know, rather than what they were taught.

Responses in the 2006 National Tests demonstrate how a focus on short-term memory, in restricted contexts focusing on 'what' and not 'why', results in learners doing exactly the above – reverting to what they think, not what they were taught. Here are some learner responses from one class:

> Question (Paper B3 b) Describe one other way that John can help stop tooth decay:
> *   Have his teeth out.
> *   Taking medication.
> *   Using toothpaste on a toothbrush.

The final answer was given the credit, but is using everyday knowledge. The first suggestion would work, but is a little drastic and was not awarded a mark!

> Question (Paper B2 dii) Why does the level of water in the saucepan go down if the water continues to boil?
> *   Because the heat is drying up the water.
> *   It's cooling down.

This question was answered incorrectly by more than half the children in the class, although this had been 'taught'. They were unable to transfer the knowledge and many learners left this question blank.

> Question (Paper B4 e) Describe how Safara could get solid salt back from the salt and water mixture.
> *   Tip the water into a sieve.
> *   By putting a spoon in and picking it up.
> *   Use a spoon and scoop out the solid.
> *   Get a spoon and pull it out.
> *   Drain it.

Nationally this was an area of weakness (QCA, 2007).

> Question (Paper A4 e) How does the earth move to cause day and night?
> *   By moving the clouds.
> *   It goes round the sun and the moon.
> *   It moves because the gravity is pulling and pushing on it.
> *   The earth moves 240 times every day and night.
> *   Because the moon moves to a different place.

This is another area that is thought to be easy but many children struggle. Once again it is an abstract idea (like dissolving and evaporating in the question above).[4]

What do they know?

If assessment is to be effective, learners need opportunities to assess their own ideas by trying them to see if they work. The starting point for this work could be a group KWHL grid, such as Figure 7.3. (What I **k**now, what I **w**ant to know (questions), **H**ow to find out and what I have **l**earnt.)

After finding out what learners know, the questions identified in the 'What I want to know' section can be placed in a question box, or on a question board. They can be used to provide homework, extension activities or as a focus for additional activities during the rest of the topic.

Focus of learning

In Chapter 2, it was suggested that when planning effective learning a clear sequence of lessons should be planned. If the level descriptions are used here to pitch the learning (Ward et al., 2005), and built into a scheme of work, time is not needed to test learners to find their level at the end of the topic (see the section of scheme of work Figure 7.4). The learning intentions should not focus only on knowledge, because learning will be enhanced by learners building their links through a range of inputs, as discussed in Chapter 3. The learning intention does not need to be the same as the outcome, which can be levelled according to the different possibilities that learners of different abilities could demonstrate. To be successful the learners are required to focus on their own development and understanding. The class has the same starting point, and learners' self-esteem is supported with the use of differentiation strategies, such as word stickers, photographs or the number or type of resource (as developed in Chapter 6). In order for learners to take ownership of their own learning and really grasp the opportunities provided by assessment for learning, they will need to develop success criteria with their teacher. Figure 7.4 shows a science scheme of work (Ward and Berry, 2006). This is just a small sample of a scheme of work which has the assessment built in.

---

[4] Using web cams from different parts of the world can help to consolidate this learning.

What I know (K)	What I want to know (W)	How I will find out (H)	What I have learnt (L)
Sounds travel well in air	How come some people can't hear?	Ask my teacher and look in a book	I know if you hit and pluck and blow things they vibrate and sounds are made
You pick up sounds in your ear drums			
Pitch is a note which sound comes in and you can have high pitch and low pitch	What are tone and pitch and volume?	Investigate and use the internet	When you hit a drum the sound travels through the middle
			A little straw makes a high sound and a big straw makes a very low sound
If you change the volume it becomes soft	What is the difference between tone and pitch?	Internet, ask and books	
Sounds travel best through gasses like air, they can also travel through some solids			Sounds travel through solid objects
	Can we measure sound?	Experiment with data loggers	Deaf peoples' ear drums do not work but they can have hearing aids
Not all sounds are the same, some are loud	Can we see sound?	Experiment	You can't see sound but you can make it splash people
I know sounds are measured in desebals			Sounds travel through materials. If you fill a bottle to the top and then fill one halfway and hit them with a spoon they make different sounds
You can make sounds using a musical instrument like a guitar			

Figure 7.3 KWHL grid for sound

Plans

Area of Science: Micro Organisms Cycle B – Lower Key Stage 2

Learning intentions	Key questions	Tasks	Resources	Outcomes	Notes
• To be able to explain findings by using scientific vocabulary	• Where do all the leaves go when they have fallen off the trees? • What happens to all the dead animals?	**Long term investigation** Children use 2L empty plastic bottles to make compost bottles. Fill with a variety of organic material (see health and safety note)	• Instructions for making compost bottles are available on the website • 2L bottles • Mesh • Tape	• Can explain findings using scientific vocabulary (level 4)	
• To be able to identify hazards and risks and take actions to control these • To be able to provide explanations for observations • To be able to use simple general-isations	• Which of these foods have changed? • Why has the change occurred?	**Classification/explore** Show children a sealed lunchbox which has been left for several days Look at which food has changed Children look at expiry dates on different foods Children compare the expiry dates of the same product that has been stored using a variety of methods (e.g. frozen and tinned peas). Children make records of their findings and offer explanations	• Sealed lunch-boxes with a variety of foods that have been left for several days • A variety of foods stored in a variety of ways	• Can make comparisons identifying similarities and differences (level 2) • Can provide explanations for observations (level 3) • Can use simple generalisations (level 3) • Can identify hazards and risks and take actions to control these (level 4)	

Figure 7.4 Scheme of work for micro organisms

CASE STUDY

Identifying success criteria

A class of Year 4 children undertook work on micro organisms. The children had been provided with a set of bags containing bread that had been treated with different substances and left to mould for ten days. The children were told the learning intention of the lesson was to make a series of observations on the amount of mould, and to provide an explanation for what they saw.

This was a child-speak learning intention and was pitched at Level 3. This is the level that Year 4 children are nationally expected to achieve. Level 1 requires the communication of observations only through words and pictures; Level 2 requires an understanding of similarities and differences (comparing the bags), whilst Level 4 would require an explanation using scientific terms.

The children, together with their teacher, decided on the success criteria, which was what the learning would look like at the end of the lesson. This included a discussion of what the learners would have in their books. Some support was needed from the teacher, as the children were new to developing success criteria and together the following was generated and written on the board:

- Have a set of drawings of the bags (4) showing the amount of mould.
- Add some words, or numbers (arrows or labels could be used).
- Write a sentence to explain which was the mouldiest.
- Write a guess as to what had been added to each bag.

The learners were then provided with the bags, rulers and magnifying glasses; they were told that the bags must not be opened. (The bags were sealed and glued to ensure they would not open by mistake!) Sets of bags were placed on tables, with the more able learners being given more bags. The children were encouraged to talk about what they saw as they worked. Less literate learners were supported with word cards and word stickers.

After seven minutes the teacher stopped the class, who were busy talking and drawing, and referred them back to the success criteria. Individual learners and the whole class were encouraged to meet the success criteria throughout the lesson. By the end of the lesson all the children had met at least three of the success criteria. They were asked to evaluate their work and then the class returned to the learning intention of the lesson. They had all made a series of observations and had provided their own explanations. The lesson finished with a short question and answer session, with the teacher supporting learners to answer some of the questions raised by their peers. The whole lesson took 45 minutes and although science was timetabled for the whole afternoon, the teacher moved the children on to another aspect of the curriculum. She found large periods of time sometimes resulted in a lack of pace. She decided the children should return to science the following afternoon, after she had looked at their work and decided how to take their learning forward. She hoped that they would progress to planning an investigation of their own, to take understanding forward. The bread bags were kept to look at later in the topic.

Continues overleaf

The teacher marked their work, providing all the children with specific feedback on it and actions to move their learning forward. This lesson showed effective brain strategies in place. The session was task focused, with opportunities to make links via the practical tasks used. The recording provided a focus for observation and discussion. Word cards and pictures supported the less able and providing more bags helped stretch the more able, who could cope with a greater number of items. The lesson was to be developed further the next day, allowing memory traces. The children loved this lesson and were happy and relaxed, thus making neuron assemblies that could be developed further throughout the topic.

Working together

For the development of learning, dialogue is important. This dialogue helps make learning happen by moving ideas from the short-term to the long-term memory. In the case of the 'How do you separate salt and water' question, all the ideas supplied can be discussed and followed up by a debate as to how these might work. This could lead to some practical work to test out the ideas. There is a view that the time where learners talk is wasted and could be used to give information or for learners to write things down. This was the approach previously favoured by the teacher of the children whose results were shared at the start of the chapter. Talk time that is well managed enables all learners to become more effective learners.

Pupils' assessment

Pupils are able to assess their own work; what they require is a clear idea of what they are learning and how they can judge if they have reached their learning goals. Learners' self-assessment is not just about them marking their work![5] They need to know what they are looking for and how they are doing so far. Helping learners to monitor their understanding through pictures which contain the key scientific vocabulary and ideas is an easy way for learners to see what they have to know. These topic specific pictures (see Figures 7.5 and 7.6) can be used again later when learners are reintroduced to key aspects. They can colour code them according to whether they have understood the ideas (green), think they know some (orange) or have no idea (red).

---

[5] *Once in maths I ticked my own work. It's not good to mark your own work because you don't know if it's right or wrong* (Y3). (Learn Project, 2000: 4).

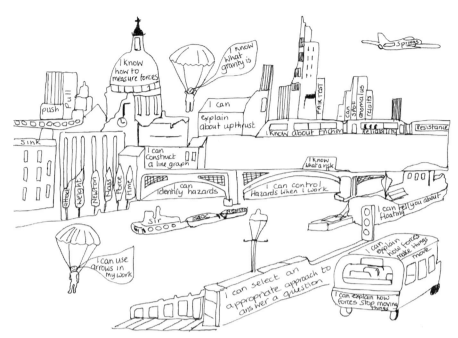

Figure 7.5 Topic specific picture on forces (Key Stage 2)

Figure 7.6 Topic specific picture on living things (Key Stage 1)

Tracking learning

If the lessons have levelled learning intentions and learners' achievement is recorded against these, it is easy to identify those who have met the learning intentions and to record the level at which they are working. Children should be encouraged to help track their progress and this will help them see the links with what they have already learned; this is most effective in helping retention and retrieval and preventing presumptions.

Returning to the KWHL grids or mind maps at the end of a topic can help demonstrate progress. Learners can add new words they have learnt, record what they now know and identify some questions they might want to learn next time they visit this aspect of science. This is motivating, builds self-esteem and is very powerful. Examples of 'before' and 'after' can be seen in Figures 7.7 and 7.8.

Figure 7.7 Light pre-teaching

In Figure 7.7 there are ten ideas represented. Understanding about absence of light is Level 2, there are some ideas showing cause and effect which would suggest a level of understanding of Level 3. Other areas of science like plant growth are found, which is useful. There are some confused ideas and no clear evidence of Level 4.

As the sun changes our shadows change

Transparent is what you can see through

You can get light from candles and light bulbs

We travel around the Sun

Light comes from the sun

The moon isn't a light source

Translucent is what you can Sort of See through

Light travels in a straight line

Opaque is what you can't see through

Reflective is what reflects things

Wasn't it there we wouldn't be able to see any light

Light can make shadows

You can see because of light, first of all round the back of your eye its upside down, but your brain makes it turn the right ways then it goes through your nerve and goes to your pupil. Thats how you see

The stars are a lot of little suns, thats why you can see them

Light helps things grow

We see because the light goes in

Figure 7.8 Light post-teaching

In Figure 7.8 there are now 16 ideas presented and some of these are linked. There is evidence of scientific vocabulary and understanding at Level 4. An understanding of Moon and light sources is clearer. There are ideas about specific light-related vocabulary. More evidence of Level 4 is demonstrated.

Summary

Assessment for learning is not about strategies and simply carrying out such strategies will not improve the opportunities for learners. Learning in science is about making links, with learners making sense of the world around them. Too much time can be spent on delivering too much knowledge, much of which is not needed; as a result not enough time is given to talking, thinking and sharing ideas. Assessment for learning is a powerful tool, as it puts the learners in control of the learning process, but it requires skilful teaching. By providing variety **retrieval** and **retention** are improved, time can appear to go faster as greater links are made, and with more neurons working together purposeful learning occurs. It is worth the time and effort.

Putting this into practice

- Avoid assessment for teaching strategies that do not involve learners in taking control of their learning.
- Provide simple feedback marking to promote self-esteem and task focused teaching, thus reducing ego involvement.
- Find out what learners know, whenever possible, and expect them to assess their own progress.
- Track learning and help learners to see how much they have learnt.

Creativity

Don't try to satisfy your vanity by teaching a great many things. Awaken people' s curiosity. It is enough to open minds; do not overload them. Put there just a spark. If there is some good inflammable stuff, it will catch fire. (Anatole France, *The Earth Speaks*)

This chapter focuses on the creative aspect of science. Often when creativity is discussed it is the art-based subjects that are thought of.

Creativity is possible in all areas of human activity, including the arts, sciences, at work at play and in all other areas of daily life. All people have creative abilities but in different ways. When individuals find their creative strengths, it can have an enormous impact on self-esteem and on overall achievement. (National Advisory Committee on Creative and Cultural Education, 1999: 7)

Recently, there has been a focus on the creative curriculum where the spotlight is more on 'how children learn' rather than 'how teachers teach'. This should help learners to think and use their brains, however sometimes the focus is more on 'topic work' and less on learners. The definition of creativity used in this chapter is 'Imaginative activity fashioned so as to produce outcomes that are both original and of value' (National Advisory Committee on Creative and Cultural Education, 1999: 31). The aim is to share examples of teaching science creatively where the focus is on learners and providing opportunities for them to be creative. Too often teaching is seen as performance art, yet it should be about learners – where they are now and how to move their progress in learning forward. Assessment, as discussed in Chapter 7, is a powerful tool in this if it focuses on the independence of learners. Creativity is also powerful when learners are enthused and believe they have skills and are valued; as a result they will display outstanding examples of creativity.

Using the above definition from *All Our Futures* can seem daunting; if originality has to be historical in nature, then noone else will have done this before. However, there is no need for learners to create a new scientific discovery. When they discover something new for themselves, this is original to them. Their work must have value to them, the setting and the task, and must not be judged in relation to that of other learners. See Figure 8.1, this is a creative response to a challenge to design a seed activity. Therefore, to be creative in science requires outcomes that are original and valuable to the learner and there needs to be a distinction between creative teaching and creativity in learning. These are not the same and this chapter is not about the creative teachers. Socrates put it so well when he said 'I cannot teach anybody anything, I can only make them think'.

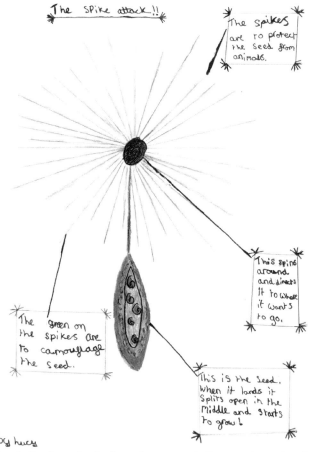

Figure 8.1 The Spike Attack. An imaginary seed dispersal mechanism. This shows the learner's understanding

Making it relevant

In the examples following in this chapter the success of the approaches was that they were relevant to the learners. The first example is from a Reception class, caring for some giant African land snails. Children were encouraged by their teacher to observe these large snails. They became fascinated by the way their 'foot' rippled as they moved. They wanted to take pictures and used the digital microscope to take moving images as well as stills. One child 'accidentally' took a picture at a magnification of 60 instead of 10. When the teacher saw the magnified picture, which looked nothing like the snail seen with the naked eye, she asked, 'What is that then?' A new game was created and other children began to use the microscope to take 'Guess what?' pictures. They used these to challenge their teacher, their friends and their parents. An interesting and exciting display was created. Language development and the observation of materials were developed at a high level. The teacher was creative because she nurtured the learners' curiosity and as a result something new was developed – and the children had fun!

Keeping ice from melting

The 'How to keep an ice cube from melting?' activity is undertaken in many schools. In order to reinforce learning a Year 2 teacher decided it was important to set a challenge – 'Who could keep the ice cube solid for the longest time?' The rules were explained. On Monday morning the children would be given a new ice cube; they had the weekend to think about the task and possibly to try out their ideas. To reinforce the learning the children were each given an ice cube in their hand as they left on Friday and were reminded it would be a new ice cube that would be used on Monday. Children left with wet hands and excited voices.

On Monday, some children had not decided what to do and they were given extra time to look at school resources and to select some for their ice cube. Other children had been helped at home. There were boxes, wrappings and containers galore, most of which were brightly decorated! One child had bought in a plastic box covered with cotton wool. The ice cubes were handed out, put into the containers and left. Throughout the day children checked their progress and recorded the time taken for the ice to melt into water. By 3 pm there was a clear winner. The child with the plastic box insulated with cotton wool won. This box was filled with frozen peas surrounding the ice cube that had hardly melted. The child explained the idea had come to him when he was out shopping with his mum. In the shop he was asked to hold the peas while his mum found a space for them in the trolley, away from everything else. He was surprised at how cold they were. Although pleased that he had won, he asked his teacher if she thought it might have been better to use peas that had been in the freezer for a week rather than a couple of days. The class then had a new challenge – to test this idea!

This activity encouraged creative responses. There were no right answers, and the activity provided a range of opportunities for registration of learning. It encouraged learners to think about and use everyday things in a different way. Parental involvement ensured that even more links were made in the brain, through questioning and extended time on task. The provision of materials in school and the time for experimenting on the Monday morning *supported* those learners who had not had support at home.

The Icemen: One to try

This will provoke a range of creative responses through using frozen plastic drink bottles. Sometimes the results are given names – the icemen, the ice trolls or the frozen ones! On each occasion learners are very enthusiastic about 'protecting and preserving' *their* iceman!

Making torches and games

This is a fun activity and one that links scientific investigation in a problem-solving way. Learners are given simple equipment and asked to use it to make a torch that works and which has a switch (Figure 8.2).

Other learners[1] were given the challenge of using the equipment to make a toy which had a Christmas theme and that had an electric circuit to make it work. The steady-hand game 'Delivering letters from the North Pole to Father Christmas' is an interesting and creative response to this brief (Figure 8.3). Interestingly, before starting on the game, learners were unsure of using electrical circuits. Making the toy, working together and using a trial and error strategy resulted in a game, which was not new but was new to them. It had value because they felt a sense of achievement when it worked. It met the success criteria and it looked good too!

---

[1] These were not primary-aged children.

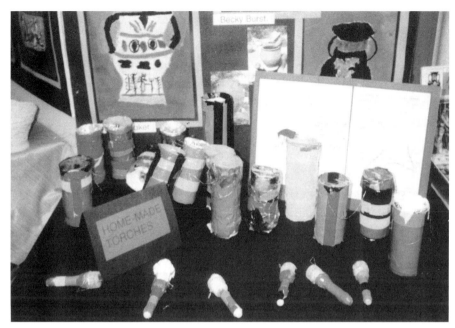

Figure 8.2 Our torches

Figure 8.3 A steady hand game

Creative responses from stories

Creative responses can be obtained from using a story as a starting point. Making links between stories and science provides a rich source for learning. It also ensures that learners who might not enjoy 'science' but like stories have the chance to get involved thus reducing rejection. Learners also get to experience learning in new settings because most story-based challenges will build on areas already covered earlier in the year. This helps to make links and to reinforce prior learning. A group of Year 2 learners was challenged to solve the problem from the story of the 'Three Little Pigs'. They tested different materials to find out which would withstand blowing a house down. One highly interesting approach was the invention of artificial wind by one group! Their wind source was an untied balloon, inflated to the same size each time. They pointed this directly at the building. It made a clever alternative from the general flapping of books and paper selected by other groups.

No right answer

> ... teachers know not only what it is they are promoting but also how to create opportunities for this to happen. Usually this means providing pupils with challenges where there is no clear-cut solution and in which pupils can exert individual or group ownership. (*Expecting the Unexpected*, HMI, 2003: 9)

Myths and legends

Using myths and legends as a starting point, a group of learners decided to investigate the sun and shadows. They made sundials, which were then tested to evaluate how effective they were at telling the time. The children thought they were not too bad for hourly intervals and worked on sunny days, but were not helpful for shorter time periods. This was discussed and one group decided they needed something for shorter times. They developed a water clock to track the passage of time spans of less than an hour.

Problems only occur if time in the curriculum is not left for such events, however if a creative curriculum is used to support such work then time can be found. In the examples discussed above the learners used language for a purpose and they measured and calculated. This approach provides opportunities to retrieve prior learning from more formal situations and to make new links in the brain; as a result retention is improved. As these are different ways of working, learners cannot develop presumptions by thinking they have done this before. They may also enjoy the activity and can often change their view of science.

Using tests

Einstein once said that his greatest gifts were stubbornness and taking seriously the sorts of questions only children ask. It is useful to see that sometimes even science test questions can be used effectively to promote creativity. One teacher working through a National Test paper with some Year 6 learners came across a question about the number of bees visiting different plants according to their colour. The children quite rightly asked if this was true or something someone has set up to test their maths skills. The teacher confessed to not knowing but suggested they should use Friday afternoon to come up with their own way of finding out.

The girls' flowers were creative masterpieces but their results were rather less straightforward to interpret than the boys'. The boys' simpler flowers still showed a difference between two of their groups. One group had cut flower shapes out of sugar paper and the other group had used plain paper and painted the flowers different colours. The sugar paper group found yellow was most popular colour and red was least popular. The results were not as clear-cut for the paint or girl groups. They posted questions on an 'ask a scientist' website and were told that the paint and glue had a smell and the insects could be attracted to things that humans would not smell at all. The feedback explained how bees 'see' light in a different way to humans. This led to some interesting creative writing about 'what the world would look like' when seen through the eyes of an insect. The learners did not have to be encouraged to learn – they were motivated, they made links, they persevered and had fun. This was an authentic learning activity and as a result new learning was developed and their understanding was deepened.

Real scientific discoveries

Aristotle noted that bees seemed to know where to find nectar and were able to communicate this to other bees in the hive. It was after the Second World War that a German scientist, Karl von Frisch, noted the dance patterns of bees and started to be interested in them. His creative mind made links between observations known for centuries and those he had registered through the observations he had made to suggest a different interpretation. It was only later (1967) that the full meaning of the dance was interpreted.[2]

Many readers will have their favourite recent scientific discovery. The awe and wonder of using nanoscience and magnetic materials to rid the blood of invading viruses is my personal favourite. A scientist developed such approaches as a result of building on ideas already retained in his brain and using these in a new and unique way![3]

Creative science in the environment

Creative science can be anything that enables learners to understand science and make a contribution. Using a picture of an environment to stimulate thinking about the needs of organisms in that environment is a common task. Providing an opportunity for learners to create their own organisms and use their imagination to extend their ideas gives them the chance to assess their current understanding, as well as introducing cross-curricular experiences.

Some children were provided with a picture of an everyday item magnified 60 times. They were then asked to decide what type of environment this was, where it would be situated, what the climate would be like. For example, was it a hot, dry place with little shade or a damp, wet, dark place? What could live in such a place? What would it eat and what would eat it? The work allowed various children to demonstrate their understanding at different levels.

Whilst some children only created simple food chains, others developed food webs and a few developed complex ecological systems. They then had to research about areas in the world to see if what they were suggesting was scientifically feasible. They also used their imagination to decide if the organisms needed to look like ones alive today or would they need to be different. Try linking this work to initiatives such as 'The Future is Wild' (www.the futureiswild.com).[4] Classroom

---

[2] It was understood that bees were able to use their ability to see light in wavelengths not visible to the human eye and were following directions given via the polarised light of the sun acting as a compass.

[3] Eric Drexler created the branch of science called 'nanoscience' and envisages making machines made of atoms that will be able to heal the human body from the inside.

[4] The concept of this site and the associated education programme is that the world has changed and will continue to change. It asks the question what would it be like without mankind intervening in the process? Scientists from many disciplines are engaged in promoting ideas based on evidence.

Figure 8.4 An environment picture which contains talktime technology which allows the children to record and retrieve information in spoken form about their animals and plants

ICT displays can also support creativity when voice recording technology is used to support learning (Figure 8.4).[5]

Problem solving and creativity

How would you get an egg across a room using only string, balloons, paper, straws and Sellotape?

If learners are never given the opportunity to use their problem-solving techniques they will lose the confidence that they can think for themselves. The number of learners who constantly ask if they are doing it right is worrying. This is not only in problem-solving lessons but also in ordinary lessons in the classroom. '*Shall I underline the title?*', '*Do you want the long date or short date?*' are some of the questions asked. Often the reason given for less problem-solving approaches is time and the lack of it; again this limits the opportunity to learn. Some questions to get learners thinking are provided below and can be used at any age.

---

[5] Talk-time technology can be used by the teacher to record information at the start of the topic. Later learners can use the technology to record their own information.

Can you build a bridge that will support the weight of 1 kg, using only paper, Sellotape and string?
Can you find out if birds can see colour?
What is the favourite food of a bean beetle?
How can you keep your hand in ice water for the longest time?

With older learners there are some fascinating, creative, problem-solving approaches which have been undertaken called the Hollywood Science Series[6]. This enables learners to investigate the science behind some famous movies and questions whether in reality these events could happen. This makes science meaningful – it gives learners the relevance in real life for science in the classroom.

What if learners had palm pilots?

Not all creative science activities require a large amount of curriculum time, just a questioning approach. How creative can learners be when given a 'What if?' question? For example, 'What if there is no gravity?'

This usually gives one or two learners the giggles when they think about some of the everyday routines and how they would be changed or be totally impossible if there was no gravity. Going to the toilet is usually one suggestion but then learners will probably suggest that there would be no toilet as they know it.

Learners of all ages can come up with 'What if?' questions of their own. They can also then start to think about what might happen as a result, for example, witness my recent MSN conversation with Charlotte.

C: '**What if**' not everything was made up of the same immutable atoms?
H: What is an immutable atom?
C: Erm.
H: Erm what?
C: I just mean an atom as in nothing can be broken down into anything smaller. But I'm rubbish at science. What if everything was made up of different elements rather than everything using the same ones, we wouldn't be able to eat animals or plant food because it would not be the same as us? And when things

ICT

---

6 www.open2.net/science/hollywood_science/

decomposed they would not be able to be used in other systems so you must have lots of waste matter?

H: I do not think you are rubbish at science, you have thought of a really interesting point. I wonder how many different elements would be needed, if they were immutable.

ICT Most school have an intranet and provide access to the internet for their pupils. Some have e-learning environments with built-in discussion boards and teachers and learners share thoughts and ideas in many formats. In Wolverhampton's local authority they are providing individual hand-held computers connected to the internet for learners.[7]

Using artefacts and objects

Providing learners with objects that they are unfamiliar with enables them to start to think about the materials involved and what they are made of, as well as what for. They can then think about why an object looks the way it does, and how the way it looks could be connected with what it does. Providing a collection of objects can challenge ideas about what things should look like and this might be a good starting point to show that not everything needs to look the same. A collection of pegs, for example for clothes, bags and the like, can promote an understanding that even amongst similar things there can be differences. Always knowing what the object is can put learners off thinking for themselves because they may get the answer wrong, but if their teacher has no idea (or says they have not) more lively and creative debates can occur. Some ideas for objects have actually been better than their real uses and can help learners to realise that 'everything comes from someone's bright idea, and maybe that someone is you'.

---

[7] Dave Whyley. 'Mobile learning for the 21st Century', www.learning2go.

Summary

- Creativity is about enabling learners to think of new things for themselves.
- New things may only be new to the learners, not necessarily new to the world in general.
- A teacher's role is to promote independence and the questioning of approaches to support learners in their development.
- Creative teachers who are performance artists might put learners off learning by being too good.
- Learners will be far more open if they think their teacher has not got an answer, and they can then stop thinking about finding the right answer and start thinking for themselves.
- ICT can support creativity.

Putting this into practice
- Provide open-ended tasks that learners know have more than one right answer and allow them time to think for themselves,
- Stand back and support learning by not doing learners' thinking for them; it might take some time for them to re-learn thinking but it will come.
- Be prepared to take risks.
- Expect the unexpected; (As with the imaginery seed activity (8.1). What did it show about learners' ability to understand plant life cycles – as well as their ability to be creative and imaginative learners?)

References

ARG (1999) *Assessment for Learning: Beyond the Black Box*. Cambridge: University of Cambridge, School of Education.

ARG (2002) *Assessment for Learning: Ten Principles. Research based principles to guide practice*. Cambridge: University of Cambridge, School of Education.

Ausubel, D. (1978) 'In defense of advance organizers: A reply to the critics', *Review of Educational Research*, 48: 251–7.

Biehler, R. and Snowman, J. (2000) 'Motivation' in M. Bloor and A. Lahiff (eds), *Perspective on Learning, A Reader.* Greenwich: Greenwich University Press.

Black, P. (2007) *Formative Assessment: Promises or Problems?* London: Kings College.

Black, P. and Wiliam, D. (1998a) 'Assessment and classroom learning', *Assessment in Education*, 5 (1): 7–74.

Black, P. and Wiliam, D. (1998b) *Inside the Black Box: Raising Standards through Classroom Assessment*. London: NFER Nelson.

Black, P. and Wiliam, D. (2005) 'Changing teaching through formative assessment: research and practice', King's Medway-Oxford formative assessment project, *English Literature Review*, 223 Formative assessment – improving learning in secondary classrooms. 92–64–00739–3© OECD 2005. Also available at: www.oecd.org/dataoecd/53/30/34260938.pdf

Bransford, J.D. (1987) *Learning, Understanding and Memory*. Belmont, CA: Wadsworth Publishing.

Brozo, W. and Simpson, M. (1998) *Readers, Teachers, Learners: Expanding Literacy Across the Content Areas* (3rd edition). Prentice Hall.

Bruner, J. (1960) *The Process of Education*. Cambridge, MA: Harvard University Press.

Cassidy, R. (2006) Radio interview broadcast on 8 October. 'Insiders' programme on ABC news. Transcript of conversation with Julie Bishop, Federal Education Minister. Available at: www.abc.net.au/insiders/content/2006/s1758091.htm

Clarke (2005) *Formative Assessment in Action: Weaving the Elements Together*. London: Hodder Education.

Claxton, G. (2002) *Building Learning Power: Helping Young People Become Better Learners*. Bristol: TLO.

Cooper, R.A., Molan, P.C. and Harding, K.G. (2002) 'The sensitivity to honey of Gram-positive cocci of clinical significance isolated from wounds', *Journal of Applied Microbiology*, 93: 857–63.

Curzon, L.B. (2000) 'Cognitive learning', in M. Bloor and A. Lahiff (eds), *Perspectives on Learning: A Reader*. Greenwich: Greenwich University Press.

Deforges, C. (2006) 'In Every Child's Learning Journey, Assessment Matters!' Paper given at AAIA National Conference, Newcastle-upon-Tyne, 13–15 September.

Doyle, C.L. (1987) 'Explorations in psychology', in M. Bloor and A. Lahiff (eds), *Perspectives in Learning: A Reader*. Greenwich: Greenwich University Press.

Dweck, C.S. (1999) *Self-Theories: Their Role in Motivation, Personality, and Development*. Philadelphia: Taylor & Francis.

Fisher, R. (1990) *Teaching Children to Think*. Oxford: Blackwell.

Fisher, R. (2005) *Teaching Children to Think* (2nd edition). Cheltham: Nelson Thornes.

Freeman, W.J. (1991) 'The Physiology of perception', *Scientific American*, February: 78–85.

Fodor, J. (1983) *The Modularity of the Mind*. Cambridge, MA: MIT Press.

France, A. (1921) *Le Crime de Sylvestre Bonnard*. Paris: Charles Henry Conrad Wright.

Friere, P. (1991) 'The importance of the act of reading', in C. Mitchell and K. Weiler (eds), *Rewriting Literacy: Culture and the Discourse of the Other*. Toronto: Oise Press. pp. 139–45.

Goldsworthy, A 'talking in science' key note address, Science co-ordinators conference. Kent LA. November 2006. Ashford International Hotel.

Greenfield, S.A. (1995) *Journey to the Centres of the Mind: Towards a Science of Consciousness*. New York: W.H. Freeman and company.

Greenfield, S.A. (2006) Report to Parliament: Education, Science and Technology. Available at: www.publications.parliament.uk/pa/ld199900/ldhansrd/pdvn/lds06/text/60420–18.htm

Greenough, W.T. (1998) 'The turned on brain: developmental and adult responses to the demands of information storage', in S.S. Easter, K.F. Barald and B.M. Carlson (eds), *From Message to Mind.* Sunderland, MA: Sinauer. pp. 288–302.

Greenough, W.T. and Bailey, C.H. (1988) 'Anatomy of memory: convergence of results across a diversity of tests', *Trends Neurosci* 11: 142–7.

Halford, G.S. (1993) *Children's Understanding: The Development of Mental Models.* Hillsdale, NJ: Lawrence Erlbaum.

Hebb, D.O. (1949) *The Organisation of Behaviour.* New York: John Wiley and Sons.

Hirsh-Pasek, K., Pulverman, R.K., Pruden, S. and Golinkoff, R. (2006) 'Precursors to verb Childhood learning: Infant attention to manner and path', in K. Hirsh-Pasek and R.M. Golinkoff (eds), *Action meets word: How children learn verbs.* New York: Oxford Press. pp.134–60.

Hubel, D.R, and Wiesel, T.N (1962) 'Receptive fields, binocular interaction and functional architecture in the cat's visual cortex', *Journal of Physiology,* 160: 106–54.

Ileris, K (2002) *The Three Dimensions of Learning.* Roskilde University Press. Denmark.

Jarvis, P. (1992) *Paradoxes of Learning: On Becoming an Individual in Society.* San Francisco, CA: Jossey-Bass.

Johnson, A.H. (1984) 'New stars for the teacher to steer by?', *Journal of Chemical Education,* 61: 847.

Kawashima, R. (2006) *Dr Kawashima's Brain Training: How Old is Your Brain?* Japan: Nintendo.

Kawashima, R (2007) 'I trained my brain', *Times2.* 15 February, pp. 4–6. London.

Keogh, B. and Naylor, S. (2000) *Concept Cartoon is Science Education.* Sandbach: Millgate House Publishing.

Lemke, J.K. (1990) *Talking Science: Language, Learning and Values.* Norwood, NJ: Ablex.

Ludwig, J. (1979) Cited in Curzon, L.B. 'Cognitive Learning', in M. Bloor and A. Lahiff (eds), *Perspectives on Learning: A Reader.* Greenwich: Greenwich University Press.

Lyotard, J.-F. (1984) *The Postmodern Condition: A Report on Knowledge* (trans. G. Bennington and B. Massumi). Manchester: Manchester University Press.

Maslow, A. (1954, 1970 2nd edition) *Motivation and Personality.* New York: Harper.

Miller, G.A. (1956) 'The magical number seven, plus or minus two: some limits on our capacity for processing information', *Psychological Review*, 63: 81–97.

Mithen, S. (1998) The Prehistory of the Mind: A Search for the Origins of Art, Religion and Science. London: Phoenix.

Morgan, M. (1984) 'Reward induced decrements and increments in intrinsic motivation', *Review of Educational Research*, 54: 5–30.

NAEYC (2003) Beyond the Journal, March, 'The Essentials of Early Literacy Instruction', available at: www.naeyc.org/resources/journal/2003/Essentials.pdf

National Academy of Sciences (NAS) (1998) *Teaching about Evolution and the Nature of Science*. Washington, DC: Steering Committee on Science and Creationism, National Academy Press.

National Advisory Committee on Creative and Cultural Education (1999) *All Our Futures: Creativity, Culture and Education*. London: DFES.

Newton, D.P. (1996) 'Causal situations in science: a model for supporting understanding', *Learning and Instruction*, 6: 201–17.

Newton, D.P. (2000) *Teaching for Understanding: What It Is and How to Do It*. London: RoutledgeFalmer.

Nissen, T. (1970) 'Indloering og poedagogik', Copenhagen: Munksgaard. In Ileris, K. (2002) *The Three Dimensions of Learning*. Denmark: Roskilde University Press.

Ogbourn, J., Kress, G., Martines, I. and MacGillicuddy, K. (1996) *Explaining Science in the Classroom*. Buckingham: OUP.

Pica, R. (2004) *Experiences in Movement: Birth to Age Eight*. Clifton Park, NY: Delmar.

Piereira, L.J. (1996) 'Stepping out with the constructivist', *Australian Science Teachers Journal*, 42 (2): 26–8.

Parliamentary Office of Science and Technology (2003) Post Note Primary science. September. London.

Pollard, A. (1992) in Craft, A. (ed), *Assessing and Planning Learning*, Milton Keynes: Open University Press.

Pollard, A. and Trigg, P. (2000) *What Pupils Say: Changing Policy, Practice and Experience*. London: Continuum.

Pollard, A. and Bourne, J. (1994) *Teaching and Learning in the Primary School*. London: Routledge in association with The Open University Press.

Qualification and Curriculum Authority (QCA) (2005) *Implication for Teaching and Learning in Key Stage 2 Science*. York: HMI.

Qualification and Curriculum Authority (QCA) (2006) *Implication for Teaching and Learning in Key Stage 2 Science*. York: HMI.

Qualification and Curriculum Authority (QCA) (2007) *Implication for Teaching and Learning in Key Stage 2 Science*. York: HMI.

Russell, T. and McGuigan, L. (2003) *Assessing Progress in Science KS1, KS2 & KS3*. York: QCA.

Senge, P. (1990) *The Fifth Discipline: The Art and Practice of The Learning Organization by Currency*. New York: Doubleday.

Smith, E. and Gorard, S. (2005a) 'They don't give us our marks: the impact of formative assessment techniques in the classroom', *Assessment in Education*, 12 (1): 21–38.

Smith, E. and Gorard, S. (2005b) 'Putting research into practice: an example from the Black Box'. Available at: www.bera.ac.uk/pdfs/ri91smith&gorard04–05.pdf

Stiggins, R. (2002) 'Assessment in crisis: the absence of assessment for learning', *Phi Delta Kappan*, 83 (10): 758–65.

Sutton, R. (2006) 'In Every Child's Learning Journey, Assessment Matters!' Paper given at AAIA National Conference, Newcastle-upon-Tyne, 13–15 September.

Waldrip, B., Knight, B. and Webb, G. (2002) 'Science words and explanation: what do student teachers think they mean'. Available at: www.sjsu.edu/elementaryed/ejlts/archives/language_development/waldrip.pdf

Ward, H. and Berry, A. (2006) *A Science Scheme of Work for Key Stage 1 and 2*. Maidstone: Kent LA.

Ward, H., Roden, J., Foreman, J. and Hewlett, C. (2005) *Teaching Primary Science: A Practical Guide*. London: Paul Chapman Publishing.

Weeden, P. Winter, J. and Broadfoot, P. (2000) *The LEARN Project: Phase 2 Guidance for Schools on Assessment for Learning Project Report* (June). QCA: York.

Wellington, J.J. and Ogbourn, J. (2001) *Language and Literacy in Science Education*. Buckingham: OUP.

Wiliam, D., Lee, C., Harrison, C. and Black, P. (2004) 'Teachers developing assessment for learning: impact on student achievement', *Assessment in Education*, 11 (1), March.

Wiliam, D. (1999) 'Formative Assessment in Mathematics: Part 1: Rich Questioning', *Equals*, Summer, 5(2).

Winkles, J. (1986) 'Achievement, Understanding and Transfer in a Learning hierarchy', *American Educational Research Journal*, 23: 275–88.

Zeigarnik, B. (1967) 'On finished and unfinished tasks', in W.D. Ellis (ed.), *A Sourcebook of Gestalt psychology*. New York: Humanities Press.

Index

A Service  rd

Trevor Lloyd
Archdeacon of Barnstaple and
Member of the Liturgical Commission

GROVE BOOKS LIMITED
RIDLEY HALL RD CAMBRIDGE CB3 9HU

Contents

The Cover Illustration is by Peter Ashton

First Impression February 1999
ISSN 0144-1728
ISBN 1 85174 394 4

1
Introduction

A Service of the Word was authorized by the General Synod in November 1998 for use from 1st January 1999 'until further resolution of this Synod.' It was originally authorized in November 1993 for use until the end of December 2000, and advantage was taken of the need to reauthorize it indefinitely so that it could become part of the core book of Common Worship, to make some changes and to add to it some parts of the *Alternative Service Book* which are going to continue in use. These include the ASB Canticles, the Litany and the so-called 'State' prayers. When *A Service of the Word* was first approved it was unique among Church of England services in that the main part of the service consisted simply of one page of rubrics or instructions. This gives a clear outline of the contents, indicating which sections of the service are mandatory and which are not. There are three pages of notes, which amplify this and include, for instance, a redefinition of the word 'sermon':

> 'The term sermon includes less formal exposition, the use of drama, interviews, discussion, audio-visuals and the insertion of hymns or other sections of the service between parts of the sermon.'

It is also unusual in having a synodically authorized three-page introduction, which explains with some care how people are to prepare *A Service of the Word*. If this is a radically different approach to Anglican worship, as the *Daily Mail* recognized when the service was originally published as part of a Liturgical Commission report *Patterns for Worship* (GS 898) in 1989, then we ought to ask both where it comes from and how genuinely Anglican it is. The *Daily Mail* (Thursday 30 November 1989) Comment column, under the headline 'Pogo sticks in every pew?' ran:

> 'Now folks for the alternative, alternative service.
>
> All those dull old Bible readings...aren't you sick of them? Okay swingers, let's put the snap, crackle and above all the pop back into gospelling.
>
> Little Jackanory-style stories from your cosy, cuddly vicar. Nothing too long. Nothing too solemn. Spotlights. Songs. Musical interludes. Exciting proclamations from soapboxes.
>
> Bags of joining in by the congregation. Plenty of movement. Don't anyone kneel or sit or stand for any length of time. You might get Christian cramp. So just keep bobbing up and down like jacks-in-the-pew.
>
> Do not adjust your *Daily Mail*, this is not some religious skit from Spitting Image, but a suitably jazzy presentation of the very latest keep-up-with-the-times suggestions from the Liturgical Commission of the Church of England's Synod.
>
> We sympathize with the predicament of the Church in this frenetic age of chat shows, fast food and two-minute attention slots.'

3

2
History

In October 1985, the Standing Committee of the General Synod published *The Worship of the Church* (GS 698), based on the Liturgical Commission's draft which was largely the work of Colin Buchanan. It said: 'The Commission suggests a programme of study and discussion, with pastoral introductions for each service, and a "directory" with a wealth of resource material, including supplementary material for each of the many points in the service where there is room for the individual's own words. The directory would need to set boundaries to the proposed freedom, and points which might be theologically divisive would have to be watched. Yet it could give encouragement to the "loosening up" which the ASB 1980 clearly had in mind but of which real advantage is yet to be taken.'

The new Liturgical Commission, beginning work in January 1986, approved a paper drafted by David Silk (then Archdeacon of Leicester) and myself, outlining proposals for a directory, which they took to the House of Bishops for approval. This saw the aims of the directory as:

'1. To provide some indication of different ways of doing liturgy, taking into account sociological, architectural and churchmanship differences.
2. To indicate where advantage might be taken of notes and rubrics in the ASB, to develop and enrich the liturgy.
3. To provide outline structures and mandatory sections for some main services, which, if authorized alongside ASB, would provide greater freedom for those who wish either to enrich or to shorten the services (including "Family" services and worship in UPAs).'

In particular, it was argued that this 'outline and resources approach' might be especially helpful in meeting the need for family services and for those who worshipped in urban priority areas.

Urban Priority Areas

Faith in the City (the report of the Archbishop of Canterbury's Commission on Urban Priority Areas, Church House Publishing, 1985, p 135) had said:
'Worship in the UPAs must emerge out of and reflect local cultures…It will be more informal and flexible in its use of urban language, vocabulary, style and content. It will therefore reflect a universality of form with local variations, allowing significant space for worship which is genuinely local, expressed in and through local cultures, and reflecting the local context…It will promote a greater involvement of the congregations in worship…It will reflect the concern of local UPA people for things to be more concrete and tangible rather than abstract and theoretical.'

4

The Liturgical Commission's introduction to *Patterns for Worship* in 1989 (p 2) indicated that these pleas had been heard: 'That report asked for "short, functional service booklets or cards," and we have provided for these. The report also asked for liturgy that promoted "a greater involvement of the congregation" and was "more concrete and tangible than abstract and theoretical," and the new writing we have done, for instance in the eucharistic prayers, is designed to meet these needs. But the needs of the UPA parish for worship reflecting local culture, language and concrete expression are not best met by a group of experts at the centre laying down all the words of liturgy, but by creating the framework and the environment which will enable a new generation of worship leaders to create genuinely local liturgy which is still obviously part of the liturgy of the catholic church.'

Family Services

Family Services had been coming in for a certain amount of attention by some dioceses. Chelmsford, for instance, had a working party, set up in 1984, which produced a very helpful report *For the Family*, which included guidelines on presentation as well as texts and examples. 73% of those who replied to the diocesan questionnaire held such services. 'In a wide range of situations, they had become another strand of Anglican worship. They are the staple, or near staple diet of a significant proportion of worshippers.' In the *Bath & Wells Diocesan News*, Nigel McCulloch, then Bishop of Taunton, wrote 'I have just been to a marvellous service. The church was nearly full—and no, it wasn't a confirmation! It was the monthly family service. The Vicar tells me it is the best attended act of worship in the village—reaching out to the less committed in a way that hasn't happened for years…Nevertheless, I do have some worries. My first worry is about the content of these family services. I have attended enough to know that, theologically, they can be very unbalanced; and that their liturgical framework is often somewhat quirky. My second worry is about those who conduct these services…The fact is that most of them do not have the authority of the Church of England to get up and deliver what, in terms of numbers present, is the main sermon of the month.'

Again, the Commission's introduction to *Patterns for Worship* contained a full discussion of the pros and cons of the 'family service,' together with a discussion of the meaning of the word 'family' and of possible titles for such a service.

The Nineteenth Century

Such services have a long history. The legal justification was the 1872 Act of Uniformity Amendment Act which was itself the result of the Joint Committee appointed in 1854, as a result of the 1851 Religious Census, which revealed the need for changes in the rules about worship in order to reach the 'unchurched millions.' The 1872 Act allowed for the shortening of Morning and Evening Prayer and for a 'third service' on special occasions, approved by the Bishop, and containing, apart from hymns and anthems, only words from the Scriptures or the BCP. This clearly did not go far enough, and in 1892 the Convocations agreed to allow the use of material which was substantially in agreement with Scripture and the *Prayer Book*. Both before and after the 1872 Act, ministers were pushing beyond the legal boundaries in order to meet the needs of the people.

At St John's Portsea, in a former circus building in 1857, experimental services were held in which 'After singing two verses of the National Anthem, the more instructive and generally interesting portions of the newspapers are read...A hymn is then sung, and a portion of the Bible read and expounded. Another hymn is sung, and a prayer offered...The meeting concludes with a doxology.' (W N Yates, *Buildings, Faith and Worship*, Oxford: Clerical Press, 1991, pp 135–6). In the great Iron Room at Christ Church, Barnet in North London, William Pennyfather invited people to what turned out to be the forerunner of the Keswick Convention, with evening mission services consisting largely of preaching, singing and prayer (though there was occasionally a communion service 'according to the form of the Church of England, of course') to which those from all denominations came. During the 1861 revival, one observer wrote 'It would be difficult to exaggerate the extraordinary visitation of supernatural power, which brought the most hardened to their knees, pouring forth a torrent of supplication which astonished experienced Christians. This had some effect on what happened in church on Sundays, with 'the introduction, Sunday after Sunday, into the General Thanksgiving, of numerous clauses, some of them most touchingly worded, from those who desire to praise God for the great spiritual mercies vouchsafed to them.' (Robert Braithwaite, *The Life and Letters of The Reverend William Pennyfather BA*, London: John F Shaw & Company, 1878, p 346).

In 1993, in *The Renewal of Common Prayer: Uniformity and Diversity in Church of England Worship*, the Liturgical Commission spelt out some of the history of the development of the Third Service, both in mission contexts, and as the result of the 19th Century Sunday School Movement, leading to examples of Children's Churches and the Family Service Movement in the mid-20th Century. In 1932, for instance, *Church Teaching for the Kindergarten* (Church of England Sunday School Institute Incorporated) produced a different order of service for every Sunday of the church's year. The Church Book Room Press produced a small booklet, *The Children's Church*, a family service based on the shortened form of Morning Prayer, and this was the fore-runner of the widely used Church Pastoral Aid Society's Family Service first produced in 1968.

The Directory

If the historical development of services to meet the needs of families and of those in urban priority areas was the most overt part of the background to the original publication of *A Service of the Word*, there was also another element in the Commission's thinking. It is not insignificant that, from the Standing Committee's report *The Worship of the Church* in 1985 and the discussions in 1986 with the House of Bishops, right up until a year before it was published as *Patterns for Worship* in 1989, the working title for this project was 'The Directory.' The change was made because of the danger of people linking it with the only other example of a *Directory* in worship in this country, the *Westminster Directory for the Public Worship of God* (reproduced as Grove Liturgical Study No 21, Ian Breward (ed), 1980), which for a period replaced the *Book of Common Prayer* from January 1644. That *Directory*, the result of a century of puritan effort to reform the *Book of Common Prayer*, consisted of an introductory historical preface, followed by instructions for each service. The first of these is clearly a word service, beginning with instructions as to how the congregation are to assemble, instructions for the public reading of the Scriptures, followed by a three-page example of public prayer before the sermon and thanksgiving after the sermon.

The Commission was grappling, as had those who put together the 1644 *Directory*, with the problem of combining common prayer with local freedom: as Ian Breward says in his introduction to the Grove edition of the *Directory*: 'It was the first attempt after the Reformation to combine order and freedom in a way that demonstrated how reform and liturgy could be profoundly unitive because it was faithfully biblical.' The failure of the *Directory* was bound up with the failure of the Commonwealth experiment, and with the fact that, as a set of liturgical instructions, it was too highly political. But it is also significant that the *Directory* played a much less important part in terms of holding the church together, simply because of the existence alongside it of the very full Westminster Confession of Faith. The confessional church of the Commonwealth era was supposedly held together by its credal statement, rather than by its liturgy. But Anglicans had become used to a lighter doctrinal statement, in the form of the Articles, with the liturgy of the *Book of Common Prayer* bearing the weight of holding the church together, exhibiting the doctrines of the faith and being the focus of doctrinal disagreements. And in the three and a half centuries since then, the *Book of Common Prayer* has done just that for the whole of the Anglican Communion.

Safeguards

So, from the Commission's point of view, if it was to move, even very tentatively, down the directory road, it was important to underline two things.

First, nothing in the directory approach of *A Service of the Word* indicates any departure from the doctrine of the Church of England. The introduction to the notes indicates carefully that all the material must either be approved by the General Synod or, in words taken from the Canons, 'neither contrary to, nor indicative of, any departure from, the doctrine of the Church of England in any essential matter.' The Synod edition of *Patterns for Worship* had, at Appendix 2, a section on the doctrine of the Church of England, containing a definition of where that doctrine can be found, which had already been used in the commentary on the ecumenical Canons, and this was reproduced in the 1995 commended edition of *Patterns* as part of a longer section on The Law and Common Prayer.

Second, it is emphasised that the move towards greater flexibility was entirely in line with the way in which Church of England liturgy had been developing. One of the aims of *Patterns for Worship* had been to draw attention to, and provide commended material for, those occasions when the ASB had provided for other

7

words to be used. These were sometimes highlighted in the introductions to the different resource sections in *Patterns*, for instance in the greeting at the beginning of the service or in the way the Confession is introduced. Douglas Jones, Chairman of the Commission in 1984 when *Lent, Holy Week, Easter* was produced, had written in the Introduction to that book: 'We are providing a directory from which choices may be made. We think of this book as a manual to be used with selectivity, sensitivity and imagination' and the book, as well as continuing the ASB tradition of allowing for variations at points within the services, had also included an outline service for the Agape with Holy Communion.

3
The Outline Structure

When the Commission were discussing what a minimal version of an alternative to Morning or Evening prayer might look like, the conclusion was that were three main elements: word, praise and prayer, plus some kind of action. The action might be something which accompanied one of the other three, such as a dramatized reading, or something which happened at the beginning or end of the service, such as lighting a candle.

This kind of structural approach had been explored by an earlier Liturgical Commission, when in 1967 John Wilkinson had written a discussion document on family services (*Family and Evangelistic Services*, Church Information Office). This brilliant little-known booklet had been intended, as Ronald Jasper's foreword makes clear, as a first step towards the eventual production by the Commission of one or more family service outlines, but the Commission's subsequent report to the House of Bishops (June 1967) simply got lost under the weight of other business.

John Wilkinson suggested a number of ways of looking at service structure, including comparison with the ACTS (Adoration, Confession, Thanksgiving, Supplication) structure for private prayer and with an approach based on the literary analysis of constituent parts of the service (what is the difference between reciting the Psalms and praying?). He suggested—predictably for a Commission member in the 60s—a four-fold shape: opening, office, prayers and conclusion. He presented these in a skeleton and in an expanded form. He also set out the theory behind the construction of the service from a series of Presentation and Response units—'a venerable liturgical pattern,' as *Patterns for Worship* was to demonstrate in showing that this is the structure of Morning and Evening Prayer. God speaks and the congregation responds—some Bible truth is presented, in a reading, invitation, song, drama, and is followed by an appropriate response of silence, praise or prayer.

Skeletons

It is but a short step from the outlines in Wilkinson's examples to the skeleton headings or one-line rubrics of *A Service of the Word*, ready to be expanded with specific and fuller material. So, in the Introduction to *Patterns for Worship* the Commission said

'...a clear structure is essential. Its main components should stand out so that worshippers can see the shape, development and climax of the service—so that they "know where they are going." It is helpful if this is reflected in the way the service is laid out for printing.'

One way of exploring the outline structure and its implications is to look at the pros and cons of having such an order. There are a number of things to be listed in its favour.

First, provided the outline is shared with the congregation in some way or other, perhaps on a service card or outline pasted into a hymn or prayer book, it offers some clarity and security to those present. They can tell where the service is going, what to expect next and roughly how much more there is to endure before the end.

Second, it enables Common Prayer, as defined in the Liturgical Commission's book *The Renewal of Common Prayer*, in providing a known and shared structure, and for some texts to be well known ones. The concept of a 'common core' is explored in the chapter by Michael Vasey, looking at both structure ('It is shape rather than particular texts that provide the common core, the "deep structure" of the major acts of Christian worship'), and also at the range of familiar words in texts. The latter will sometimes belong to the core 'because of their place in the structure of the rites; others gain their place in the core because of the affection they inspire.' This concept of the common core is a development from the argument expressed in the introduction to *Patterns for Worship*:

'"Common prayer" does not in fact exist, in the sense of being able to walk into any church in the land and find exactly the same words to follow. Nor should we pretend that it would be either good or right to return to a position—well over a century ago—when that might have been the case. Rather, "common prayer" exists in the Church of England in the sense of recognizing, as one does when visiting other members of the same family, some common features, some shared experiences, language and patterns or traditions.'

Third, it enables each service, or the regular service in each locality, to be tailor-made to each local cultural situation. At most points, no texts are specified and therefore choice can be made among the material that is available, or something new and specific to the local situation can be written. But, while material which arises out of and speaks into the local cultural situation is encouraged, clear limits are set. There are four possible categories of material, which can be seen if we ask some questions.

- What are those points in the structure where something—the same thing, perhaps—should always happen? There should always be a greeting, for instance, but not necessarily always in the same words: 'The minister welcomes the people with the greeting.' But no words are specified; any can be used. The position, but not the text, is mandatory.
- What are those points where any text (or none) can be used? Neither the position nor the text is mandatory, for example in 'Venite, Kyries, Gloria, a hymn, song, or a set of responses may be used.'
- What are those perhaps more sensitive points where, for the sake of the unity

of the church in terms either of its doctrine or its corporate memory, it is important that the same words are used? Look for the word 'authorized' which means text approved by the General Synod under Canon B2, and you will find you can only use authorized words for the Confession and Absolution and for the Creed or Affirmation of Faith. But both of these can be moved, though only in a limited way: 'Authorized Prayers of Penitence may be used here or in the Prayers.' And the Liturgy of the Word section is followed by a line saying 'This includes' and then a list of things which includes 'an authorized Creed, or if occasion demands, an authorized Affirmation of Faith.' This gives an indication that though this list of things occurs at this point, it need not be in this particular order.

- There is nothing in *A Service of the Word* in the final category, when both text and position are mandatory.

Fourth, the 'skeleton' and 'flesh' approach enables the General Synod to determine very easily those points at which the church needs to be united on agreed texts, and those points where variety is acceptable. A simple proposal to insert the word 'authorized,' or for an amendment to change the word 'authorized' to 'suitable' is all that is needed. In future, we may reach a point where it is only really essential to use the lengthy and costly liturgical business process for authorized structures and particular authorized texts.

Fifth, this approach enables ancient and modern texts to be used easily in the same service. One of the problems of the 1974 Worship and Doctrine Measure and the arrival of the ASB and its preparatory booklets was that PCCs were forced to choose between a wholesale modern language and structure approach, and staying with the *Book of Common Prayer*. If all you have is a series of headings, texts can be chosen which provide more variety, or the possibility of more gradual, piece by piece, movement towards a modern text.

Norms

Further, there should be some long-term advantage to the worshipping life of the church in setting down the norms. Every act of worship which is clearly alternative to one of the statutory services, whether family service, mission service or for a special occasion, should have a structure which falls within these norms, and includes some standard Anglican elements. The fact that a service includes a few such elements may help it to be a better bridge for those who may be moving to more standard 'mainline' Church of England worship. In *Patterns for Worship*, the Commission had tried to answer the question: 'What is it that makes our worship specifically Anglican?'

'We believe that some of the marks which should be safeguarded for those who wish to stand in any recognizable continuity with historic Anglican tradition are:

- a clear structure for worship
- an emphasis on reading the word of God and on using psalms
- liturgical words repeated by the congregation, some of which, like the creed, would be known by heart
- using a collect, the Lord's Prayer, and some responsive forms in prayer
- a recognition of the centrality of the Eucharist
- a concern for form, dignity, and economy of words.'

Problems

There is, of course, a flip-side to all this. What are the problems of a skeleton and flesh approach?

- It could lead to a lessening of doctrinal control over the church's worship. Creating a situation where lay people are not sure, because of the large variety of texts now usable, whether what the minister is using is an authorized text could open the door to doctrinal confusion. Perhaps awareness of this will simply underline the need for the church to exercise doctrinal discipline, for example over preaching or approaches to pastoral work, in some other way than depending on the church's liturgy.
- It could lead to totally variable mix-n-match worship every week. There are few churches which could cope with this and one would hope that, perhaps after trying such a programme for a few months, the leadership of the church (whether the vicar, the worship planning group or the PCC) would see that this was not the best approach. In any case, if the provisions of *A Service of the Word* are observed, the structure at least should be similar one week to that of the previous week.
- This approach to worship is more demanding in terms of the time taken to prepare. Like most of the Common Worship material, it is not possible simply to take the book off the shelf, go into church and use it. And it not only demands more time in preparation, but also gives an opportunity for something else which is demanding in time, namely to involve other people in the preparation of worship, and in the process to teach them both about worship and about relating to God.
- It might result in very poor material being used, though this raises questions as to what criteria are being used to judge the quality of the material: is it poor in terms of the local culture, or is it poor in the eyes of some middle class person coming in from outside? And the flip-side of this is the encouragement of creativity. There is clearly a need to establish ways of sharing new material, to engage in mutual criticism and to provide workshops at the local deanery level where examples can be shared and standards discussed.
- It could appear to give a licence to produce a service which is simply a chorus-sandwich style of entertainment, with different groups 'putting on their bit' with little sense of direction. The Commission was very much aware of this danger, and produced on page 25 of *Patterns for Worship* a set of ten guidelines, which include these two:

'How much of the service might be classed as "entertainment"? Is this justified? Is there a balance between receiving (listening, watching, contemplating) and responding? Check on posture: is there too much sitting down or standing up at one time? Is there enough action?'

'Is the structure and direction of the service clear enough for people to know where it is going? Does the service have an overall coherence, or is it just one entertainment item after another?'

One of the novel features of *A Service of the Word* is that it has a three-page Introduction which was authorized by the Synod. This describes the structure of the service and offers hints and tips on how to put a service together. It ends:

'Once the service is planned, leaders will want to check through to ensure there is a right balance between the elements of word, prayer and praise, and between congregational activity and congregational passivity. Does the music come in the right places? Is there sufficient silence (Note 4)?...And is there a clear overall direction to the service: is it achieving its purpose...?'

So there are enough warnings around, in Guidelines, Introduction and Notes, to steer people away from the entertainment package.

Movement and Flexibility

Those planning such a service should have some idea of the movement within it, and in particular whether it is moving towards some climactic point. In some ways it does not matter too much what this is, so long as there is some clarity about it; and indeed it may vary from service to service. It would be possible to see the climax of the service in the reading of the Gospel, the preaching of the sermon, or in the intercessions, as the response of faith—the living sacrifice of the church in prayer, responding to the Word proclaimed and preached.

The structure is sufficiently flexible to allow for experimentation with different ways of doing things. The difficulty is that we are rightly averse to the thought of changing the structure from week to week, as that might destabilize the worship pattern, and we are also sometimes bound by our own expectations and experience to accept the standard pattern because that is safe. Three examples of possibilities for adventure are there in the text. In the Introduction to *Patterns for Worship* we read:

'In making the distinction between the Service of the Word and the Breaking of Bread, between the first and second parts of the Eucharist, we should allow for a pattern to develop where there is a sufficient break between the two parts (perhaps with an extended Peace, with or without refreshments!), for those enquiring about the Christian faith and baptism to go without embarrassment, at the end of the Service of the Word.'

13

This is based on the ancient pattern when 'the catechumens (those preparing for baptism, however old they were) were excluded from the Eucharist. Their formal departure at the end of the Word Service would have been a dramatic feature of the liturgy in a large building, probably involving some upheaval in the congregation as a whole.' In the two hour service at Holy Trinity, Wealdstone in the 1980s and 90s, the teaching element was emphasized, sometimes with adults as well as children going out for their own groups immediately after the readings; sometimes intercessions happened in these groups, and sometimes in church, but then everyone came back together for the Peace, which included refreshments and lasted for 15–20 minutes, making the point that fellowship is an essential part of our worship together. This provided for some to depart at this stage, and for the eucharistic thanksgiving and prayer which followed to be a coming together and summing up, not only of the Ministry of the Word, but of the many concerns which had been voiced during the time of fellowship.

It is not necessary to assume, for instance, that each part of the service must follow on immediately after the previous one. Note 3 indicates that the outline provided may be interrupted by Hymns, Canticles, Acclamations and the Peace. It would be quite possible to have a service where an identical Acclamation, repeated at stages in the service, acted as an indicator of the structure, as well as ensuring that everyone was both awake and up to speed on where the service had reached.

Another possibility is indicated in Note 7, which not only allows the Sermon to come after any of the readings (so that the exposition closely follows the reading of Scripture) but also allows for more than one sermon, with sections of the service coming between them. This potentially more dramatic structure might , for instance, be used if a story was being told, to which the different sections of the service might act as a response.

4
The Contents

1. The Holy Communion

As part of the Liturgical Commission's early thinking in preparation for *A Service of the Word*, there were discussions about the relationship between the Word Service and the Office.

This is summarized in pages 10–12 of *Patterns for Worship*. There are three ancient strands:

* the Word Service (the first part of Holy Communion), described by Justin as consisting of readings from the prophets or Apostles, 'read for as long as time allowed,' followed by a 'discourse,' and common prayer;
* Daily Prayer (Morning and Evening Prayer), consisting of praise to God at certain times of the day in fixed psalms, hymns and songs, plus intercession, with, later on, many introductory prayers, the continuous recitation of the Psalter, and readings from Scripture of ever-increasing length, distorting the original simplicity; and
* the Teaching or Instruction referred to in Hippolytus' *Apostolic Tradition*, possibly a direct offspring of the synagogue service, a Bible study with no particular liturgical shape.

'As history proceeds, these three types of service, which major respectively on reading the word, on prayer and praise, and on teaching, do not remain distinct.'
and so
'...we would want to argue that "word-services" of different structures should be regarded as an interchangeable first part of Holy Communion.'

In line with this, the first (Synod) edition of *Patterns for Worship* in 1989 included not only some experimental eucharistic prayers but also a 'Form of Service for the Holy Communion, Rite C,' together with 'Instructions for the Eucharist.' The latter survived into the commended edition of *Patterns* in 1995, and provides an excellent three-page introduction to eucharistic structure. But Rite C, the outline communion service, proved to be too great a risk for the House of Bishops to take. When *A Service of the Word* was eventually introduced to the Synod the covering report said 'the Commission has been asked by the House of Bishops to bring forward its proposals for a Service of the Word separate from other, eucharistic proposals in *Patterns for Worship*.' However, it had attached to it a table amending Section 47 of ASB Morning and Evening Prayer and showing how *A Service of the Word* could be combined with Holy Communion—'a logical extension of providing for the Service of the Word to be a substitute for Morning or Evening Prayer.'

A SERVICE OF THE WORD

In 1979 the *Book of Common Prayer* of the Episcopal Church in the United States
had 'An Order for Celebrating the Holy Eucharist' which was an outline order,
'not intended for use at the principal Sunday or weekly celebration of the Holy
Eucharist.' This consisted of instructions and headings, together with two outline
eucharistic prayers which included extempore thanksgiving and only spelt out
the text for the opening dialogue, sanctus, narrative of institution and the prayer
immediately after that about remembering and for the Spirit, followed by 'The
Celebrant then prays that all may receive the benefits of Christ's work, and the
renewal of the Holy Spirit.' When in 1996 'Holy Communion Rites A and B Revised' was introduced into the Synod, the Revision Committee had this short
American rite in front of them, with the suggestion that it should be added, to
replace the provision in *A Service of the Word*. The Committee used this text, suit-
ably revised, in order to provide 'Outline Orders' at the beginning of the services
'to give a clearly expressed "overview "of the shape of the rite which is to follow.'
But it declined to propose 'an authorized order for the eucharist which comprises
no more than an outline' particularly because that would add a fifth rite to the
four already being proposed. It did, however, suggest pursuing the proposal in
the context of the renewed authority for *A Service of the Word*, and published a
version of the outline order on which it had worked, as part of its report, curi-
ously entitled 'Trevor Lloyd's Minimal Format Version' (*Eucharistic Rites A and B
in the Alternative Service Book: Report of Revision Committee*, GS 1211Y, Church House
Publishing, 1997).

So when the Revision Committee for *A Service of the Word* set to work it simply
took over this outline, inserted section headings to make it even clearer, and amal-
gamated the Notes with those for *A Service of the Word*. It was, in any case, necessary to change the old provision relating to Section 47 in the ASB services of
Morning and Evening Prayer, as that would no longer exist in the Common Worship core book. In any case, the Committee took the view that this outline order
for the Holy Communion should be seen as an integrated whole, rather than
encouraging people to see it as an 'add-on' to Morning or Evening Prayer.

This is now an extraordinarily flexible rite—hence the warning that it needs
careful preparation—and only three items are marked with an asterisk to indicate
that an authorized text must be used: confession and absolution, the Collect and
the Eucharistic Prayer. The Creed is not mentioned, being included under 'The
People and the Priest proclaim and respond to the Word of God,' but Note 8
indicates that sermon and the creed or an authorized Affirmation of Faith may
not be omitted on Sundays. Note 5 on Readings says that where this version is
used on Sundays and principal Holy Days, the readings of the day are 'normally'
used—but even in that word there would appear to be a measure of flexibility. As
Note 10 says 'The order provided is not prescriptive,' and no words are prescribed,
for example, for Breaking the Bread or the distribution of communion. It is interesting to reflect that this is currently the only Church of England Communion
Service, apart from that in the *Book of Common Prayer*, authorized into the new
millennium. It also has the effect of legalizing the continued use of Rite A (so long

16

as the Penitential section comes at the beginning), but not Rite B (where the Confession comes in the middle and where the Breaking of Bread need not be a separate section). It may, as is often the case, be some time before the Church wakes up to what the Synod has done, but for those who are aware of this outline, there will not only be some freedom, but possibly the growth of a spiritually and linguistically rich alternative eucharistic tradition.

2. The Notes

The Revision Committee, in their *Report*, say 'In general it is recognized that, for *A Service of the Word*, Notes and rubrics are a combination of prescription and advice. Bearing that in mind, care has been taken over the use of words such as "may," "might" and "could."' An examination of these words—and also 'if occasion demands'—will reveal the very real amount of flexibility that exists. In Note 1, on the Greeting, the main point is that the service should have a clear beginning, and the Greeting may come after some introductory singing or a sentence of Scripture, and be followed by a prayer or an introduction to the worship. And the Greeting is defined as 'liturgical,' partly as a result of Hugh Craig's speech when the service was first debated in Synod in 1995:

'When I go to a church service which starts off with the vicar or reader saying Good morning to me and with my being meant to say Good morning to him, I find it a total turn-off for real worship. One of the advantages of old-fashioned things like the *Book of Common Prayer* is that they start by trying to draw the attention of the worshipper to God. I very much hope that section 1 will be revised in such a way that whether or not A says Good morning to B, the predominant feature of the beginning of the service is doing that which will turn men's, women's and children's minds to God and his Word and his reality—unless we do that, the rest will be in vain.'

A salutary reminder of the spiritual purpose of the opening part of the service!

Note 5 deals with Readings, and 'if occasion demands' allows for a service with only one reading, and sets out a slightly longer period of what the lectionary calls 'Ordinary Time' than that in *Calendar, Lectionary and Collects* (Church House Publishing, 1997). It runs from the Third (rather than the First) Sunday in Advent to the Baptism of Christ, and from Palm Sunday (rather than Ash Wednesday) to Trinity Sunday, perhaps indicating the rather more flexible approach of this service. The norm, when combining *A Service of the Word* with the Eucharist on Sundays, is to use the set readings, but even this is governed by the word 'normally' and by Note 6 to the Lectionary which indicates that 'after due consultation with the Parochial Church Council, the minister may, from time to time, depart from the lectionary provision for pastoral reasons or preaching or teaching purposes.' No doubt proper advantage will be taken of this for such things as preaching series of sermons during Lent or majoring for a few weeks in the Family Service on the goriest Old Testament stories.

Note 7 contains a historic redefinition of the Sermon to include 'less formal exposition, the use of drama, interviews, discussion and audio-visuals.' The Revision Committee explored the alternatives (address, talk, etc) but felt it was clearer to retain the old title and expand its meaning. Whether this will have an effect on those who run sermon classes in theological colleges and courses and Reader training courses remains to be seen…

3. Confession and Absolution

Note 2 indicates that only authorized Prayers of Penitence may be used. The 1993 Revision Committee for *A Service of the Word* (*Report*, GS1037Y, p 7) 'acknowledged that the wording of absolutions has been a matter of controversy in the past and many look for some guarantee that only authorized forms are used at this sensitive point.' Yet the committee also felt that to restrict the forms to those in the *Book of Common Prayer* and the ASB would be too narrow, especially as alternative forms of confession and absolution had appeared in seasonal services commended by the House of Bishops. So it was decided to include an appendix with a number of forms—it turned out to be sixteen in the end—of both confession and absolution. They were drawn from *Patterns for Worship* and from commended services such as those in *The Promise of His Glory*. Their various sources, and the changes made by the Liturgical Commission, are discussed on pages 20–22 of *Introducing Patterns for Worship* (Trevor Lloyd, Jane Sinclair and Michael Vasey, Grove Worship Series No 111, 1990). It was the 1993 Revision Committee which took the decision to put 'us' as well as 'you' into the forms of absolution, italicized to show that 'us' could be changed to 'you' and vice-versa, but with a random number of texts with either pronoun. This was a recognition, not only that many of these service might be led by lay people, but that in some circumstances those in priest's orders are increasingly using the 'us' form.

Little change was made to this section by the 1998 Revision Committee, despite an impassioned plea during the Revision Stage debate in July 1998 to change the word 'abuse' in the responsive confession on the theme of the cross: 'We run away from those who abuse you,' on the grounds that this word could nowadays only mean one thing. A brief examination of the response to this suggestion shows the detailed care taken both in compiling the original and in considering the suggestion. A number of points were made:

- To change it would encourage the narrow sexual interpretation of this word, though that can be justified from the Old Testament (eg Judges 19.25). Against this, professionals working in this area increasingly see abuse as not just sexual but emotional and verbal as well as physical. All of these are involved by implication in the use of the word in this line.
- This Confession follows a careful pattern, from the betrayal in line 7 through the mocking and beating of the soldiers to Peter's denial in line 19. The line in question refers to the incidents described in Matthew 26.67, 68, both to words covering the mocking and striking Jesus when blindfolded (the word *paisas*

may mean 'playing') and also to the word *ekolaphisan* meaning 'to violently maltreat.' It is not easy to find one word which covers this range of emotional and physical maltreatment; 'abuse' does that, whereas 'ill-treat' is weak.

* When Peter refers to this incident in 1 Peter 2.23, he uses the word *loidoroumenos* which might be translated 'reviled.' Both the RSV and the NRSV translate this 'when he was abused...'
* The word also conveys some of the overtones of Isaiah 53.5, and an assonance with the word 'bruised' in that verse.

4. Affirmations of Faith

This contains two sorts of material. First, there are versions of the historic creeds, including a responsive version of the Nicene Creed, where the length of the responses gets shorter towards the end as it moves towards a climax, and the short alternative baptismal creed, now brought into line with the slightly longer text in the Initiation Services. There is also the question and answer version of the Apostles' Creed, used on the Pope's visit to Canterbury Cathedral in 1982 and first published in *Lent, Holy Week, Easter*, and a translation of the christological portion of the Athanasian Creed, first drafted by Michael Vasey. There is nothing like translations of the creeds to get theological debate going—something for which most Revision Committees are ill-equipped—and here it centred on the lines originally drafted in the Commission's 1989 text as:

Fully God and fully human;
one human person with mind and body.

The Revision Committee—against the advice of the Steering Committee—felt the second 'human' was redundant 'since our Lord's personhood adheres to both his human and divine nature' and went for 'one person with mind and body.' The Latin is *'perfectus deus, perfectus home ex anima rationabile et humana carne subsistens,'* translated by J N D Kelly, the authority on the creeds, as 'perfect God, perfect man composed of a rational soul and human flesh.' What the Revision Committee had done, in an error caused partly by the lack of clarity in the Commission's translation, was to stress the 'one' when the first line did all that was needed for unity and balance between humanity and Godhead, and to omit the human aspect which was essential for the second line. After discussion at the Revision Stage in Synod, this was one of those rare instances when the House of Bishops changed the translation, as a result of correspondence between the Steering Committee and the Bishops of Birmingham and Ely, so that it now reads:

Fully God and fully human;
human in both mind and body.

The second group of Affirmations are credal excerpts from Scripture, originally reproduced in *Church Family Worship* (ed. Michael Perry, Hodder and Stoughton,

1986). The one from Ephesians 3 was added by the 1993 Revision Committee.

Between these two groups is the credal hymn 'We believe in God the Father.' The Commission had discussed the possibility of authorizing one or two credal hymns as part of its proposals, but concluded that even something like Newman's 'Firmly I believe and truly' was too far away from the text of any of the creeds. As chairman of the Commission group responsible for *Patterns for Worship* I wrote to ask Bishop Timothy Dudley-Smith if he could write a metrical version of the Apostles' Creed which could be sung to a standard hymn tune. 'We believe in God the Father' was duly written in August 1989, and not only sticks amazingly closely to the original but conveys a certain beauty and grandeur as well.

5. ASB Canticles and Prayers for Various Occasions

For the sake of completeness, we ought to note that when *A Service of the Word* was approved by Synod in 1998 it had attached to it not only Prayers of Penitence and Affirmations of Faith but two sections of the ASB which were uncontroversial and which would need authorization beyond 2000 in order to be part of the core book of Common Worship. The ASB canticles fall into three groups. First, those where there is an agreed international ecumenical translation, an 'ELLC' (English Language Liturgical Consultation) text. While there is a general presupposition, agreed by Synod, that the ELLC texts will be used, there were a number of proposals for change. Changing the word 'he,' when referring to God, to 'God' does not seem too obtrusive in the Benedictus, but does in the Magnificat, so the Revision Committee restored the 'he' in two places. In the Te Deum, while agreeing to insert 'the' in the second line (We acclaim you as the Lord) for the sake of euphony, the Committee kept 'you humbly chose the Virgin's womb' despite criticism that this language is not strong enough to convey the 'you did not abhor' of the *Book of Common Prayer*.

The second group are two psalms used as canticles, Psalms 95 (Venite) and 100 (Jubilate), for which the Committee used the latest version of the revision of the American Psalter being produced by the Commission for the new book. It also omitted the verse from Psalm 96 imported by the ASB and restored the full text of Psalm 95, with a note to say it could end at verse 7.

The third group includes some slightly more modern canticles, together with the Easter Anthems and the Song of Creation. The latter attracted the most changes, and is now in two forms: a shorter form with the refrain after each verse, and a longer form following the pattern of the Franciscan Office Book (*Celebrating Common Prayer*) where the refrain comes less frequently.

Prayers for Various Occasions includes the Litany, the 'State Prayers' and Endings and Blessings.

Among the suggestions for improvement was one asking for the reinstatement of the petition for women in childbirth. After consultation with the Mothers' Union, the Family Life and Marriage Education council and the Board for Social Responsibility this petition was put firmly in the context of family life:

Bring your joy into all families;
strengthen and deliver those in childbirth,
watch over children and guide the young,
bring reconciliation to families in discord
and peace to those in stress.

The Revision Committee removed the title 'State Prayers' as it was thought inappropriate for such a varied collection of prayers, and provided a separate title for each prayer. There is one new prayer here, written by the Steering Committee, for 'Those who govern,' which prays for 'Elizabeth our Queen...the parliaments in these islands...and...the members of the European Institutions...'

5
Creative Possibilities

Baptisms and Funerals

If the skeleton-and-flesh approach can be seen to work both for the Word Service and, by extension, for the Eucharist, would it help to apply the same principles to other services? The Liturgical Commission's proposals for Funeral Services have a similar outline (not skeleton!) order, consisting simply of rubrics which show the order in which things happen and where an authorized text is necessary (for prayers of commendation and committal, for example). This provides a looser structure for funerals which may be necessary on particular occasions, such as the funeral of a child or a baby, without having to provide a worked-out service intended to cover all occasions and ages. The Commission were advised against doing the same thing for the Marriage Service because of its statutory position, but have proposed an outline service, followed by a worked-out example, for a service for the Renewal of Marriage Vows. These would seem to have all the advantages described above, of encouraging good locally-produced services for special occasions which nevertheless share a common structure, together with the use of some key authorized texts. This approach also makes demands on the initial and continuing training of clergy in liturgy, for which better provision must be made.

When the *Common Worship Initiation Services* were published (Church House Publishing, 1998) they included both the one-page authorized set of rubrics and instructions for the Baptism of Children at *A Service of the Word*, and also a fully worked-out service with the same title showing how it might be done. There are no Prayers of Penitence at the beginning, the baptismal Profession of Faith replaces the Creed, and there is an option to use some of the introductory material in the Baptism service as part of the Preparation section of *A Service of the Word*. The main texts of the Baptism service come after the Liturgy of the Word, and are followed by Intercessions and the Ending.

Other Services of the Word

Working on the same principles the Liturgical Commission is constructing other worked-out versions of *A Service of the Word* for possible inclusion in the core book of Common Worship. These might include, for instance, the equivalent of ASB Morning and Evening Prayer, which are authorized by the approval of *A Service of the Word*, as well as Family Services and (possibly) Compline. The only problem with Compline is that a sermon is required on Sundays—and of course the traditional Compline form of confession is not one of those authorized in *A Service of the Word*.

The last page of the document which authorized *A Service of the Word* authorized a schedule of changes allowed in the text of the *Book of Common Prayer* services of Morning and Evening Prayer, so that these could appear in the Common Worship in the forms in which they are commonly used, for example abbreviating 'Dearly beloved brethren…' and omitting the first of the two Lord's Prayers.

There is a slight question about how far the authorization of *A Service of the Word* also authorizes daily office forms such as that in *Celebrating Common Prayer*. There does not have to be a penitential section in the CCP office, but this is mandatory in *A Service of the Word* on weekdays as well as Sundays. The various places for canticles, acclamations and responses are all allowed for by Note 3, and putting the psalm before the readings is also no problem as the items in the Liturgy of the Word section can come in any order. The CCP Sunday office would have to include a Creed or Affirmation of Faith to stay within these provisions. And the Lord's Prayer is mandatory in *A Service of the Word*, but optional in the CCP office. So, apart from Penitence and the Lord's Prayer, most of what is needed is in place. It remains to be seen whether the forms of daily office to be proposed by the Commission do in fact fall within these guidelines, or will need separate synodical authorization.

Mission Services

In the last century, as noted above, it was the evangelistic zeal of some church leaders which led to some softening of the services imposed by the Act of Uniformity. Now, as then, the more energetic will probably use forms, liturgical or not, which go beyond the bounds of the strict legal requirements. But that does not make it less important to have such boundaries; the provisions of *A Service of the Word* are intended to state what the norms of liturgical worship are. They will have a good and useful effect if they provide some kind of expected structures for those evangelistic or mission services which are intended to take place in church and to lead people towards the regular worship of the church. They will act as a bridge in this way if they retain some of the structure and elements of regular worship.

But there are also many evangelistic occasions, sometimes in church, sometimes not, which are really presentations of the gospel in preaching, drama, song, interviews and visuals, where there might be a couple of hymns and a prayer but the whole thing is not basically worship, and so in no way falls under the provisions of the Act of Uniformity about public worship. Those planning such presentations ought perhaps seriously to ask whether in including a couple of hymns and a prayer they are embarrassing non-Christian visitors by putting words into their mouths about adoring and following Jesus Christ. There is the same problem about the mandatory Creed or Affirmation of Faith in a mission occasion of a slightly more churchy nature, based on *A Service of the Word*.

Such a mission service might take full advantage in other ways of the outline and Notes, like this, for example:

- Welcome and scene-setting: why are we here?
- 'Scriptural song,' perhaps a solo to set the mood, or to ask questions.

23

- Drama: a contemporary situation relevant to
- The Reading, perhaps with audio-visual backing.
- Sermon, part 1.
- Perhaps another song, and some interviews or a video clip.
- Sermon, part 2.
- Creed: perhaps the short question and answer one, or 1 Corinthians 15.3-7 ('Christ died for our sins...'). People might be challenged as to whether they could say this.
- Intercessions, which could be very brief and include a prayer of commitment, followed by
- Conclusion...

Conclusion

This example simply demonstrates how difficult it is to be outside the law! But, more importantly, it shows two other things. First, the flexibility of the order and the ability to include a wide variety of items with in the service. There is plenty of scope, for instance, for the Family Service which majors on one story and lets it invade every area of the liturgy, and for the inclusion of a large number of seasonal variations. Second, one of the real benefits of *A Service of the Word* is that it encourages those who plan worship—and perhaps congregations too—to pay attention to structure and how the service develops. This may make great demands on us, and many mistakes will be made, but there will be clear rewards for those who plan and take part in our worship in the years ahead.